17/41.

£4.50

Ge

Feminist ferment

introductions to history

Series Editor: David Birmingham,
Professor of Modern History, University of Kent at Canterbury

A series initiated by members of the School of History at the University of Kent at Canterbury

Feminist ferment

"The woman question"
in the USA and England,
1870–1940

Christine Bolt
University of Kent

UCL
PRESS

First published in 1995 by UCL Press

UCL Press Limited
University College London
Gower Street
London WC1E 6BT

and
1900 Frost Road, Suite 101
Bristol
Pennsylvania 19007-1598

The name of University College London (UCL) is a registered
trade mark used by UCL Press with the consent of the owner.

British Library Cataloguing in Publication Data
A catalogue record for this book is available from the British Library.

Library of Congress Cataloging-in-Publication Data are available.

ISBN: 1-85728-382-1 PB

Typeset in Sabon and Gill Sans.
Printed and bound by
Page Bros (Norwich) Ltd, England.

Contents

Acknowledgements

I should like to express my sincere thanks to Rosemary Clarke-Jones and Joan Hill at the University of Kent: to Rosemary for typing the text of *Feminist ferment* with such interest, speed and eye for detail; and to Joan for producing different versions of the bibliography with her customary dispatch. I am also most indebted to the three anonymous assessors of the project for UCL Press; and to its Senior Editor, Steven Gerrard; the Senior Production Editor, Sheila Knight; the copy editor, Anne Rafique; and the indexer, Isobel McLean.

My focus in *Feminist ferment* has been the United States and England, not Britain, though it is not always easy to separate the English and British women's movements. In an introductory work, this focus has been adopted because of space limitations and because most scholars have devoted themselves to English feminism. The endeavours of Scottish, Irish and Welsh activists are at last beginning to receive the attention they deserve in the writings of, for example, Cliona Murphy, Rosemary Owens, Leah Leneman, Eleanor Gordon and Angela John.

But that is another story.

Christine Bolt
July 1995

Acknowledgements

Introduction

When feminists first met in America in 1848, they looked ahead to "no small amount of misconception, misrepresentation, and ridicule" (Seneca Falls Convention Report). They were true prophets. Feminism has been seen as a threat to men's comfort, family values and social stability. Its achievements have been contested, its female adherents denounced as mannish, its male supporters as effeminate. Feminists have been presented as divided over ideas and goals, unrepresentative of women, and at once alarming and inconsequential. Pronounced dead several times, feminism still survives, and the judgements upon it of our own day inevitably colour comments about past feminist campaigns. The complexity and contentiousness of this important social movement make it a rewarding subject for students of protest and reform, and for those interested in the position of women in a changing world.

By 1870, nationally organized women's movements had emerged in the United States and England, and they had been encouraged in each country by a similar range of factors. The growing importance of women in Protestant sects, which strengthened feelings of sisterhood, led some pious women to religious benevolence and ultimately to activism on their own behalf. As the nineteenth century saw the advance of industrialization, urbanization and class formation, a number of middle-class women began to see reform endeavours as a defining characteristic of their class. Being largely excluded from the new industrial jobs, which went to their poorer sisters, they were none the less determined to assert their influence by tackling the

1

problems that accompanied economic upheaval. Moreover the British and American commitment to extending political rights and permitting pressures for change from outside the legislature allowed protesters of various kinds to spring up, though they enjoyed very varying degrees of success.

Important ties also bound the United States and Britain generally, especially for the first half of the nineteenth century, buttressing the sense of common interest felt by feminists in the two countries. Britons and Americans were linked by the same ancestral stock, religion, language and system of common law, while an Atlantic economy developed in trade, capital and labour, and a parallel exchange of ideas and visits evolved between American and British humanitarians, Nonconformists, evangelicals and political radicals (Thistlethwaite 1959). But the differences between Britain and the United States were as great as the similarities, with activists being very conscious of them and of their own distinctiveness.

The United States came into existence declaring the right of its citizens to be free from a tyrannous British monarch and a British people "deaf to the voice of justice and consanguinity" (Declaration of Independence, 1776). During the decades that followed, diplomatic relations were frequently strained, particularly before and after the Anglo-American War of 1812, and as a result of Britain's ambivalent attitude to the ultimately victorious North during the American Civil War of 1861–5. Major disputes between the United States and Britain were, however, mostly settled to American advantage, and the American conservatives who retained an open admiration for British culture and achievements found themselves a declining force in the nineteenth century. As early as 1776, the radical pamphleteer Thomas Paine had urged American colonists to revolt, with the reminder that they inhabited a rich continent peopled from around the globe and not just England. By the 1820s, the United States had committed itself to a generous immigration policy that made naturalization easy and helped to tempt across the Atlantic successive waves of increasingly diverse immigrants. And if many found poverty and racial injustice in the New World, they continued to come in search of opportunity and in the belief that America was a *different* country.

Such an impression was confirmed by the relatively healthy environment of the United States, by its comparatively youthful and educated population, and by the ease with which its inhabitants moved westwards, constructed a transport network, exploited their abundant domestic resources, adapted the technology of Europe to their needs and, in the North at least, fashioned a highly successful economy geared to market forces (Bagwell & Mingay 1970). Foreign visitors invariably remarked upon Americans' irrepressible pleasure in present achievements and firm faith that they had an exceptional destiny in the world. National imperfections could even be admitted without embarrassment by the many citizens who believed that the United States was far more committed than Britain to the spirit of reform, from which, in the 1841 words of the New England intellectual, Ralph Waldo Emerson, no "town, statute, rite, calling, man, or woman" could escape (quoted in Griffin 1967).

In Britain, whereas radicals might derive pleasure from the American enlargement of liberty, achievement of political democracy, and separation of church and state, more numerous and more critical voices were raised from the late eighteenth century, expressing unease about the purposes, pretensions and potential of the new republic. The Revolution had impelled such Britons to reconsider the viability and inviolability of empire, made them more self-consciously patriotic, and stiffened their determination to see strong government at home and abroad (Colley 1992). For the next few decades, as the United States survived and grew, it was possible to take comfort in ridiculing the hypocrisy of Americans who claimed moral superiority over the British while sustaining chattel slavery and removing resisting Indian peoples from their ancestral lands. It was likewise possible to denigrate the Americans' underdeveloped culture and overdeveloped interest in the almighty dollar. Despite its leaders' desire to assert a distinctive policy towards Europe and the Americas, most famously expressed in the Monroe Doctrine of 1823, the United States was felt to rely on British power to back up its claims. The British Empire had clearly survived the loss of the American colonies: indeed, Britain was confident enough to loosen its grip on its white dominated outposts from the 1840s. Meanwhile, it was established as the centre of international finance, more industrialized and urbanized than the United States, and advantaged by a sounder currency and cheaper labour.

Yet in the period between 1865 and the First World War, the picture changed inexorably. The British reform acts of 1867 and 1884 reduced Anglo-American political differences but, if anything, strengthened conservative Britons' fear of importing the progressive features of American life. Because the extraordinarily speedy industrial and urban transformation of the United States was accompanied by strains and injustices that pro-business government only exacerbated, radical elements in Britain also became critical of their former idol. To make matters worse, America – behind tariff walls and with a more rapidly expanding population – had emerged as the world's major economic player, whereas Britain's share of world trade, on which its prosperity depended, had declined. And the increase in Anglo-American diplomatic co-operation from the end of the century reflected as much Britain's need for allies, and the rise of America's power and interest in the world, as it did a sense that the two leaders of the so-called Anglo-Saxon race were united in their basic characteristics and objectives.

The Anglo-American relationship was thus a significant one for both countries but fraught with difficulties: a shifting combination of understanding and incomprehension, nostalgia and hope, friendship and rivalry. It is against the background of this relationship that the closely connected English and American women's movements must be understood. They were to prove equally complex and prone to change, and their ideas and biases, organizations and leaders, campaigns and opponents, which will now be examined, played a part in revealing and challenging the essentially male national identities carefully forged on each side of the Atlantic during the nineteenth century.

Throughout this study, such nineteenth-century terms as the woman question and the women's rights movement will be used alongside such twentieth-century terms as feminist and feminism, for convenience and in order to stress what I believe to be the vital continuities in women's activism. I accept, of course, the distinctiveness of feminist endeavours in the nineteenth and twentieth centuries, but contend that in both periods feminists were concerned with analysing the nature of womanhood; highlighting the disabilities women suffered as a result of customary definitions of femininity; establishing at once their individuality and their shared concerns; and working for improved educational, economic, domestic, political and legal rights.

Comparative studies of women's movements are not numerous and each has its own distinctive focus. Accordingly, William O'Neill's pioneering study of England and America (1969a) is notable for its illumination of the distinction between reformist and equal rights feminism, and its stress upon the strength of the former in the United States. Richard Evans (1977) has traced the activities and varieties of organized feminism in Europe, America and Australasia. Olive Banks (1981) has charted the main Anglo-American feminist traditions from 1840 to the present; and Jane Rendall (1985) has paid particular attention to the social contexts in which feminism emerged in Britain, France and the United States. It has been my intention in this and my earlier study of British and American feminism (Bolt 1993), to do equal justice to the two movements and to question the frequent American claim to exceptionalism (Vann Woodward 1968). I have tried to point up the difficulties feminists encountered in seeking to establish the universality of sisterhood. I have endeavoured to show what factors have contributed to the successes and failures of women's movements, while highlighting the distinctive features of women's experiences in the two countries that led international feminism from the 1870s to the 1930s. And I have seen English and American feminists as being engaged in what scholars call social movements: in other words they were able to articulate beliefs, mobilize people, sustain a search for social change, and deploy organization without it becoming their defining feature.

CHAPTER ONE
Ideas

It seems important to begin with the ideas of the women's movements. In the first place, many of them had been floated well before feminists made their organizational breakthrough in an era of economic upheaval and reformist pressures. And secondly, notwithstanding the circulation of recognizably feminist arguments since at least the eighteenth century, the unsympathetic are much more likely to recall the feminists' leaders, behaviour and campaigns than they are to remember their ideology. If they can rehearse feminist ideas, they will probably be aware that these have divided women from women, as well as from men – and still do. Yet in the nineteenth century, women who hoped to change the treatment of their sex began by debating what they were and wanted, on paper and at meetings. They, like other reformers, believed this to be the best way of attracting supporters, converting opponents, and keeping their cause alive when action proved difficult. Unfortunately they, like other busy and practical reformers, seldom left full or regularly updated expositions of the ideologies thus produced. The proceedings of the women's gatherings were not always preserved and feminists frequently concentrated on reporting "news": that is gains and defeats, events staged, members acquired and contributions received. Just the same, in their organizational records, journals, pamphlets, speeches, letters and books (including memoirs and imaginative literature), the feminists have left an absorbing account of their intellectual odyssey.

Since women's mental inferiority to men was widely assumed, it was necessary to demonstrate women's ability to reason and challenge conventional thinking. In shaping their arguments, questioning English and American women might draw inspiration from the fact that, whereas their daily lives were subject to customary and legal constraints, their minds had remained free; and that being able to resist spiritual bondage, they could go on to oppose its practical forms. Furthermore, by the 1870s, feminists in each country had their own particular advantages. American women had benefited from the national belief that the extension of democracy and primary education must go together if the republic's citizens were to be fitted for their duties. It was consequently deemed essential that the mothers and prospective mothers of the republic's citizens should be sufficiently instructed at the primary and secondary levels to act as teachers, at home and in the classroom. The feminists who emerged in the United States before the Civil War were usually well educated, and this was one of the factors that gave Elizabeth Cady Stanton and Lucretia Mott the confidence to call together the founding women's rights convention in 1848, at Seneca Falls in upstate New York. Galvanized by the success of the Seneca Falls meeting, for the next twelve years American feminists found their most notable outlet in regular conventions, which afforded them the opportunity to clarify their own and their opponents' ideas. In England, where feminists did not organize until the mid-1850s, women were more rigorously instructed for their class position, and there was no republican fillip to educational provision. But they gained assurance from having played a distinguished part in producing the literature of an established culture, and from the stronger tradition of assemblies in private homes: salons that brought together the fashionable, politically active and intellectually prominent of both sexes.

The root cause of feminism is the perception that women and men are physically and mentally different, and that their innate and divinely sanctioned differences warrant the enforcement of separate spheres for the sexes. This conviction gained strength from the idea that, in its fundamentals, the position of women was the same the world over and had been the same throughout history. If many commentators alleged that the treatment of women in progressive Britain and the United States was superior to that in less civilized parts of the world, they did not question the differences between the sexes and

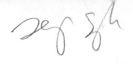

the institutional arrangements that accompanied them. Indeed, during the first half of the nineteenth century, as industrial capitalism separated home and workplace, especially for the middle class, while a cheaper press and higher literacy levels enlarged the reach of anxious moralists, there was an increase in sermons and advice manuals dwelling upon women's special characteristics and extolling the merits of the domestic sphere. In that sheltering sphere, it was argued, women should be accorded increased powers as the guardians of society's values, children, the family, health and tranquillity amid the turbulence of modernity. Conversely, men were to rule supreme in the intellectually and physically demanding public sphere of politics and war, paid work and high adventure. Such views and those who held them are considered in Chapter 4; they are introduced here simply to emphasize that feminism did not develop in an intellectual vacuum and was perforce reactive or adaptive as well as original in its ideology.

Feminists employed several novel arguments. They insisted that the supposedly separate domestic and public spheres actually overlapped, with men being in a position to dominate both. They maintained that these spheres were not natural but man-made creations, and hence open to challenge and change. While venerating motherhood and domestic duties, they rejected the notion of women having a single destiny resulting from their biological function. Instead they held that women were diverse and rational individuals, who were entitled to the same human rights and opportunities for self-development as men. On the one hand, feminists were innovative in conceding that women could be rendered subservient through social and psychological conditioning. They were innovative in presenting their dependence on men as a denial of their humanity and a form of bondage, rather than as an honourable burden borne by men for the good of all. On the other hand, feminists reacted with prudent adaptability to their contemporaries' stress on the opposing qualities of the sexes. They did so by highlighting the allegedly natural female traits that they could turn to their advantage. Accordingly feminine piety, dutifulness, maternalism, sympathy and practicality were said to give women a special moral authority – some even claimed superiority – that required their participation in the domestic and public spheres alike. Female assertion could thus be seen as unselfish: beneficial to society as a whole and not simply women, and involving no threat of a sex war, since male and female roles remained complementary.

When making their case, English and American women were also able to borrow from a number of intellectual developments that preceded the emergence of organized feminism in the 1840s and 1850s. Eighteenth-century Enlightenment thought, if only marginally concerned with women, was generally helpful to them in its libertarianism, and specifically in its celebration of the rationality of all human beings; the possibility of their progress; the existence of natural rights guaranteed by natural law; and the importance of education. The primacy of the individual's search for salvation in the Protestant religion, which was dominant in England and in the United States, had always been useful to women, who suffered from the elevation of institutions and authority figures in other faiths and in the secular world. But they had further benefited, by the early nineteenth century, from the undermining of the severe dogmas of Calvinism by sectarianism and revivalism, and from the emergence of an evangelicalism that prized feeling and good works, traditionally associated with the female sex. In addition the liberal creed, which was the eventual political expression of Enlightenment rationality and the Protestant ethic, had a relevance for feminism (Evans 1977). Admittedly, its exponents were male and the individualism it extolled had a competitive emphasis that was at odds with the normal expectation that women would serve others rather than themselves. Nor was its early support for limited government appealing to those feminists who favoured a more interventionist state to tackle injustice. However, women could first exploit liberalism's belief in progress, personal autonomy, equality before the law and government based on consent, and then utilize its eventual emphasis on social altruism to press for women's enfranchisement, and for acceptance that injustices in the domestic sphere were not a private matter but properly subject to public debate and political intervention (Shanley 1989).

Just as English and American women fashioning feminist ideas were assisted by their own distinctive social conditions, so they had their own ideological emphases. In the United States, arguments about equality were buttressed by references to the nation's founding Revolution, whose leaders had begun by claiming the rights of Englishmen, formalized through the Glorious Revolution of 1688, but had ended by claiming universal human rights. Ironically, the constricting celebration of femininity and domesticity was likewise stronger in the United States, because of the receptivity of its developing culture to new intellectual fashions; the exaggerated veneration given to women in areas (such as the western territories) where they were in short supply; and the comfort that could be derived, in a constantly changing country, from the belief that women, at least, lived stable lives within the family. Since the established Anglican and Congregational churches had been disestablished after the Revolution, and Protestant sects forced to compete for members had been glad to draw in women, American feminists built upon their position of strength by boldly challenging the claim that their subordination was authorized in the Old and New Testaments. These texts, they urged, had been misinterpreted by men and hence misapplied in church organization. Echoing the famous ex-slave activist, Frederick Douglass, who had distinguished between the religion preached by Christ and that practised by southern slaveholders, intrepid American women throughout the nineteenth century avoided the patriarchal in favour of the democratic message of the Scriptures. A collective venture, *The woman's bible* (1895), conceived and driven to publication by Mrs Stanton, was the feminists' most famous effort to elucidate biblical pronouncements on women, and the critical response the project aroused led the veteran Stanton to reiterate her "demands for justice, liberty, and equality in the Church as well as in the State" (Stanton 1898; Lerner 1993).

Finally, feminists in the United States made much of the analogy between racial and sexual slavery. Women, like slaves, had been denied individuality, choice and full adulthood; and they too, if married, lacked a legal identity. Under the common law of coverture that prevailed in the two countries in the early nineteenth century, husband and wife were legally one person and that person was the husband. As a result, in the absence of an expensive pre-nuptial contract and in return for her husband's commitment to support both her and her children, a married woman lost control of the property she brought to marriage or acquired after it, including wages. She was also denied the power to sue or be sued, and to carry out legal transactions, as well as lacking sovereignty over her person, children and domicile. American women had proclaimed this slavery of sex from the 1830s, a period of social and intellectual ferment favourable equally to an assault on slavery and the emergence, first of female reformism and then of feminism. In Britain, although women had been prominent in abolitionism before their American sisters, it had not usually led them to feminism. Slavery had been ended at home and in the colonies by 1833, and while Britons continued to denounce the survival of servitude in other parts of the world, they accepted profound class divisions within British society. Under these circumstances, middle-class female abolitionists in Britain tended not to feel that their own status was directly undermined by slavery, however much they saw it as a general threat to family ties and an affront to the sensibilities of all women. Nevertheless, by the 1870s the British anti-slavery campaign was in comparative decline, and some of its female members did feel able to deploy their old rhetoric in the new women's movement (Sklar 1990; Midgley 1992). In one of the ironies with which history abounds, the alliance between American abolitionism and feminism had simultaneously ended in acrimony, the slaves having been freed and black men enfranchised after the Civil War, whereas their female allies had been denied the vote by a Congress unwilling to tackle two risky issues at once (DuBois 1978).

English feminists, organizing from the 1850s to the 1880s in a less democratic yet proudly progressive country, felt obliged to develop a strain of calculation and expediency at the outset. They commonly presented their arguments in connection with the specific parts of their campaign that they wished to advance, keeping contentious issues separate and carefully using such comparatively radical spirits as the Unitarian MP's daughter, Barbara Leigh Smith-Bodichon. In similarly pragmatic fashion, they made the most of the worldwide publicity given to the exposition of *The subjection of women* (1869) by the Liberal MP and political philosopher, John Stuart Mill. Mill's work was utilized by feminists on each side of the Atlantic because of the fame of its author; his unusually warm acknowledgement of the intellectual inspiration he had derived from his wife, Harriet Taylor; and his outspoken views. Offering a searing indictment of female subordination under contemporary marriage laws, Mill argued that women had the right to develop themselves fully as free individuals in a world that was no longer dependent on masculine might. Rejecting notions of women's physical or natural weakness, and believing that society had mostly denied them the opportunity to demonstrate their intellectual potential, he maintained that both sexes would benefit from ending women's unjust and outmoded inequality. In particular, men would no longer exercise unearned and corrupting power, and they would better enjoy the close relations imposed by the conjugal family, while women would become less narrow in outlook as they were able to put their faculties to the "higher service of humanity". What is more, having been brought up "equally capable of understanding business, public affairs, and the higher matters of speculation, with men in the same class of society", women might expect that the "pleasurable enjoyment of life" would replace the "weariness, disappointment, and profound dissatisfaction" that were so often their lot (Mill & Mill 1970).

The official view of their powerful ally among England's feminists was the one offered by the *Englishwoman's Review* in 1873. In a leading article in July of that year, the journal paid tribute to Mill's various activities helpful to the cause, concluding that his thought had "taken root in thousands of women's hearts, and . . . the work he began will be carried on by eager assistants till it is finally accomplished" (no. XV). Women activists were none the less aware that Mill had not tackled some crucial questions that they were willing to confront, both in public and private (Caine 1992). Persuaded that women were always likely to favour "the one vocation in which there is nobody to compete with them", he did not give sufficient attention to women's need for greater economic opportunities, without which they were obliged to seek matrimony as their principal employment. And he paid scant regard either to the rights and wrongs of working-class women or to the positive bonds of womanhood (Mill & Mill 1970). The application of liberal theories to the condition of women, by one of their leading exponents, clearly revealed the limitations, as well as the value, for feminism, of any pre-existing ideology. Undaunted, English feminists engaged in lobbying politicians for reform invoked the tenets of liberalism as ingeniously as they could, and were influenced by a strong vein of radicalism running from the work of the eighteenth-century polemicist, Mary Wollstonecraft, through to the writings of the early nineteenth-century utopian socialists, whose arguments on behalf of the complete emancipation of women remained influential in the 1850s, together with a number of their veteran exponents (Taylor 1983; Rendall 1985, 1994).

The basic ideas of the organized women's movements, like their programmes, emerged very quickly. But feminism also developed

13

over time, taking account of the shifting composition of the movement, alterations in women's circumstances, challenging opportunities, and intellectual developments in society as a whole. A number of
historians have maintained that the American activists, having initially based their case upon equal rights theory, came in the later
nineteenth century to stress expediency or functional arguments
(Flexner 1959; O'Neill 1969b; Banks 1981; Kraditor 1981; Buechler
1986). In other words, they asserted that women should have the
vote, enter the public realm, and generally shed their fetters, because
when they did, they would be able to apply valuable feminine
attributes beyond the home. This modified emphasis is explained in
terms of feminism's detachment from its Enlightenment and anti-
slavery roots, and its recruitment, once it became more respectable,
of growing numbers of conservative women who favoured the functional approach, having seen its effectiveness in justifying and
expanding women's involvement in reform. It is admitted, however,
that functional arguments were always used and equal rights arguments never abandoned by American feminists. And there was obvious wisdom in devising a woman-centred appeal that drew in
supporters and reassured men, even while it suggested that their rule
had produced innumerable social evils that emancipated women
might properly tackle. Feminists in England, despite their prudence,
always asked for changes as of right, as well as for the good they
could do with them. Yet they, like their American sisters, could see
the value of focusing on women's special morality, given the influence in both countries of social Darwinism: that is the application
of Charles Darwin's biological findings to the social order by the
English philosopher, Herbert Spencer. The Spencerian idea that the
highest forms of life were the most specialized was used to dignify
the divergent roles of men and women (Conway 1980).

One of the most difficult areas for women to tackle on either side
of the Atlantic was sexuality, though contrary to the view of early his-
tories of feminism, it was a subject that keenly concerned them from
the first (O'Neill 1969b; Rover 1970; Smith-Rosenberg 1985; Leach
1989; Kent 1990; Simmons 1993). In the United States by the 1860s,
debate had been sparked by awareness of the growth of prostitution,
abortions and the incidence of divorce; in England, the galvanizing
factor was a campaign against state regulation of prostitution in
targeted towns, undertaken from the end of that decade against a

background of concern about the spread of venereal disease (see Ch. 5). Feminist thinking here was not original but, once again, it shrewdly adapted prevailing opinion for novel purposes. The central goal, declared the American feminist, Caroline Dall, was "to demystify women's sexuality" (quoted in Leach 1989). While neither women nor the medical profession were united about women's commonly alleged lack of pleasure in sex, the initial feminist appeal was for limiting sexual intercourse within marriage, so that motherhood was voluntary and men made to practice the self-control expected of women. Such an appeal reinforced the image feminists liked to project of women as the moral sex, was designed to end the double standard of morality for the sexes, and offered practical assistance to married women otherwise exposed to the risks of repeated pregnancies in an age before reliable means of birth control were available. Furthermore, celibacy could be genuinely applauded in single women, rather than demanded but pitied, since it allowed them to devote their energies to social betterment and demonstrate their emancipation from the sexual indulgence associated with "lower orders" and "lesser breeds" (Gordon 1976; McLaren 1978; Weeks 1981; Showalter 1992). It was part of the feminist indictment of marriage that women forced to pursue it were, in the words of the radical American writer, Charlotte Perkins Gilman, led to an exaggeration of "sex-distinction", with the "over-sexed woman" so limited in her interests as to act as a brake on every kind of progress (Gilman, 1966; Kent 1990).

The feminist elevation of sexual restraint broadly prevailed until the interwar years of the twentieth century, and from the 1870s justified women's involvement in social purity and social hygiene campaigns designed to improve public morality and protect mothers and children (see Chs 5 and 6). The maternalist strain in feminism that resulted was also encouraged in the same period by the eugenics movement, which supported state intervention to control the population and encourage the "right" people to reproduce. However, ideas about the denial or management of sexual activity did not go unchallenged. In the middle and at the end of the nineteenth century, before the First World War and during the 1920s, awareness of social change prompted some feminists to commend sexual emancipation, not control. The emancipation they favoured was often the freedom simply to discuss sexual matters frankly, but by the twentieth century feminists' outspokenness in this area was matched by their greater boldness in asserting women's right to work outside the home, and to marry or not as they chose. Feminists' frankness was made still more alarming by being linked to their long-term interest in health and dress reform. Just as women were to be strong-minded rather than intellectually quiescent, so they were to be physically strong. Accordingly, feminists maintained that women themselves could best understand their own bodies, and that once such knowledge was widely disseminated, could improve their own health independently of the male dominated medical profession. Although the role of the state in promoting public health had greatly expanded by the First World War, women as individuals could still strike a blow for liberation by taking exercise and rejecting the constricting garments dictated by fashion. And such free spirits might be emboldened by the writings of sexologists who believed that sexual expression was necessary for men and women alike, as well as by the growth of socialism, a few of whose adherents had always questioned customary attitudes to matrimony, birth control and sexuality (O'Neill 1967; Weeks 1981; Reed 1984; Jeffreys 1985; Showalter 1992; Taylor 1992).

Sex radicals constituted a minority in the women's movements of both countries. The hostile reaction to Mary Wollstonecraft's unorthodox sexual and political life may have inhibited the appearance of like minds in England until the utopian socialist efforts to create experimental communities between the 1820s and 1840s, whereupon one of the outstanding publicists of that cause, the Scottish-born author and reformer, Frances Wright, encountered conservative criticism on each side of the Atlantic. When in the turbulent Civil War and Reconstruction era a number of American feminists, most notably the adventurous sisters, Victoria Woodhull and Tennessee Claflin, took an interest in free love, the response was once more bound to deter emulation. In England during the 1870s and 1880s, the sexual unconventionality of women like the socialist advocate of birth control, Annie Besant, and the suffragist, marriage reformer and social purist, Elizabeth Wolstenholme Elmy, was rare. Between the 1890s and the First World War, such feminists again remained uncommon, though they found some sustenance in, for example, the Men and Women's Club and *Freewoman* magazine in London, and the Heterodoxy Club and Greenwich Village district in New York

City. Yet what they meant by free love was a considered not a careless stance: that is, the voluntary union of women and men based on affection, designed to endure with that affection but free from the intervention of unjust marriage laws and the obligation "to marry to escape destitution", which was "clearly sexual slavery" (quoted in Alexander 1988; Sochen 1972; Rowbotham 1977; Jeffreys 1985; Bland 1986; Schwarz 1986; Cott 1987; Leach 1989; Showalter 1992; Taylor 1992; Holton 1994a; Mason 1994; Bland 1995).

As the American suffragist, Laura Ellsworth Seiler, saw it, free unions were taken more seriously in England than in the United States, something that "reflected, of course, the much more difficult position of women in England than in America; American women have always had more freedom" (quoted in Gluck 1985). While her judgement was widespread among American feminists, it needs substantial modification. With specific reference to sexual attitudes, British women certainly exercised their early lead as novel-writers to raise questions and depict feminine behaviour that threatened established stereotypes. Hence we find them regularly presenting women as prostitutes, wayward adolescents and alarming orphans, alongside sexless creatures destined for the safe haven of matrimony. And in the 1860s "sensation" novels by authors such as Rhoda Broughton, Mrs Henry Wood and Mary Braddon, there are middle-class female protagonists whose restlessness, independence, active sexuality and even criminality led to public protests from commentators accustomed to think of women as domesticated angels. The fact that some men also wrote sensation novels was no reassurance, and nor were the unconventional personal circumstances of their key exponents, in a period of sensitivity about urban problems, a rising crime rate, and a sensationalist press. The intent of these novels might not be overtly feminist, and no fiction should be read as a straightforward reflection of women's actual lives; but the anxieties they aroused were fed by feminism and helped to prepare the way for the "new woman" fiction of the 1890s (Showalter 1978; Helsinger et al. 1983; Flint 1993; Reynolds & Humble 1993).

The "new woman" genre, unlike the "sensation" novel, is to be found in the United States as well as Britain, and to be understood in the context of social developments that were dismaying to a range of groups. These developments included the changing position of women, an expanding industrial order, municipal mismanagement, a declining birthrate, increasing immigration, competitive imperialism, and a general *fin-de-siècle* dread of regression and chaos. As had the writers of the 1860s, the novelists and dramatists of the 1890s portrayed women in a subversive fashion. Often assertive, they questioned their upbringing and instruction, the state of matrimony and motherhood, and the sexual double standard. Modern commentators have pointed out that the female "new woman" authors – among them Sarah Grand, Mary Dunne ("George Egerton") and Olive Schreiner, an influential South African feminist who for a while participated in British suffragism – found it especially difficult to break away from the accepted ideas about feminine sexuality, picturing its expression as an isolating, painful and unhappy business. They plainly recognized that a gap still existed between their aspirations and the reality of women's lives. This awareness did not prevent them from looking ahead to an ideal world of sexual equality, and utopian visions were particularly prevalent among American "new woman" novelists, including Charlotte Perkins Gilman, Elizabeth Corbett and Marie Howland (Showalter 1978, 1992; Coslett 1988; Ammons 1991; Gardner & Rutherford 1992; Flint 1993; Reynolds & Humble 1993). Such visions were encouraged in the United States by the enormous success of Edward Bellamy's utopian novel, *Looking backward, 2000–1887* (1888). Bellamy's projection of a co-operative social order appeared just when the excesses of the industrial economy had become disturbingly apparent. It prompted the foundation of clubs throughout the country to spread Bellamy's ideas and proved appealing to women, who were among the chief victims of unregulated capitalism (Buhle 1981).

It is hard to know how far the "new woman" fiction influenced individuals towards feminism. It was strongly denounced by conservatives, which may have deterred timid women from considering its message. Equally, anything fashionable may be read merely out of curiosity, and some older feminists expressed qualms about the wisdom of jettisoning old ideals of womanhood. But the nineteenth century had witnessed a steady increase in concern about what women read, as a consequence of improved female education, the enhanced leisure of middle-class women, their greater determination to earn a living as writers, and the growth of publications by and for women. By the twentieth century these included the plays and novels written by the innovative British suffragists and not matched by American activists; and journals like the *Englishwoman's Review, Victoria Magazine, Women's Suffrage Journal, Shafts, Votes for Women,* and *Suffragette* in Britain; and *Woodhull and Claflin's Weekly, The Revolution,* the *Woman's Journal* and *Equal Rights* in the United States. If such periodicals included all kinds of material, they nevertheless dealt with the "woman question" in a measured way, reviewing significant works of literature and providing copy that was designed to make their readers think seriously and question. The "new woman" fiction handled feminist issues in a less didactic and coherent manner, despite the active suffragism of some of its exponents, notably Grand, Schreiner and Gilman (Showalter 1978; Stubbs 1979; Rosenberg 1982; Spender & Hayman 1985; Rubinstein 1986; Ammons 1991; Caine 1992; Flint 1993). Yet women were important consumers as well as writers of literature; and the controversial "new woman" novels reinforced the explicitly feminist message contained in the journals and suffragist fiction. All three kinds of writing seem both to have made an impact and to have helped build up that sense of community among women that was vital to the progress of the feminist campaign.

Most significantly, the "new woman" literature drew attention to the fact that the feminists' critique of the family had grown more insistent than ever. Contrary to the view that once prevailed among historians, who were misled by the caution of most early activists on birth control and divorce, feminists had complained from the first about women's constraint under the marriage laws, their lack of time for themselves inside the family circle, and the limited alternatives to matrimony. By the end of the nineteenth century they were, in addition, stressing the link between sexual matters and women's family role, and confronting the variations of that role according to class. Initially the focus had been on the bourgeois family, with middleclass feminists worrying about finding and keeping the good servants whose work set them free, and arguing that service could be rendered a more attractive occupation through the provision of training and through fortunately placed women paying their servants a fair wage. At the 1848 Woman's Rights Convention in Rochester, New York, Mrs Stanton had pointedly urged "the necessity of reformers commencing at home" (Report, 1848). In time, however, feminists had turned their attention to the vulnerability of working-class women as they struggled to make ends meet, combine work in and beyond the household, and raise children in frequently unhealthy environments. As working women became increasingly reluctant to labour as servants, some middle-class activists of mainly socialist and Darwinist bent urged the reform of housework, which they saw as unprogressive and unspecialized. And in asserting women's right as well as need to work outside the home, feminists investigated the ways in which work and the family had interacted more helpfully in bygone times, eventually challenging society's aversion to the employment of married women. In this part of their argument, no less than in others, they were anxious to use the past as well as fashionable contemporary theories to their advantage (Schreiner 1911; Gilman 1966; O'Neill 1969b; Degler 1980; Basch 1982; Hayden 1982; Stetson 1982; Dyhouse 1989).

Notwithstanding their skill in developing a feminist ideology, the women who devised it faced some embarrassing and intractable difficulties. In the first place, since feminism has encountered fierce opposition, women have been nervous about describing themselves as feminists, or about doing so wholeheartedly. Because the women's movements often campaigned around single issues in both countries, it was easy to be a convert on a topic that appealed, without embracing the cause as a whole. Yet on all the key issues of feminism, activists disagreed, reflecting the diversity of the female population as a whole and the tendency of ideological disputes to occur as social movements mature and look ahead (Buechler 1990). With regard to the family, feminists differed over whether they wished to reform or radically reconstruct the institution: over whether it was women's strongest base or biggest oppressor. As a result, they did not, in the main, challenge the prevailing division of labour within the home. A similar divergence existed on sexual questions, with some feminists asserting women's right to an independent sexuality, but more being of the opinion that freer relations between the sexes were likely to disadvantage women in terms of pregnancies out of wedlock and social disapproval. If this customary prudence paid dividends, it also inhibited the discussion of lesbianism before the 1920s, leaving the field primarily to sexologists who, in the late nineteenth and early twentieth centuries, labelled lesbianism as a socially and psychologically damaging form of "pseudosexuality" or unconscious repression. In so doing, the "experts" helped to sexualize and discredit singlehood just when the numbers of unmarried women seeking employment and companionship were increasing on each side of the Atlantic (Chambers-Schiller 1984; Jeffreys 1985; Smith-Rosenberg 1985; Leonardi 1989; Simmons 1993).

More broadly, activists assumed the universality of sisterhood, springing from women's shared characteristics, socialization and grievances. But they were at first primarily comfortably placed women using arguments that had currency in the circles from which they came. Much as the abolitionists had done, when commenting on African-Americans, feminists claimed women's supposed inferiority was the result of an unfavourable environment, not innate qualities. Unfortunately, their parallel acceptance of women's distinctive nature pushed them towards the intellectual position of anti-feminists who, encouraged by the findings of nineteenth-century science, equated biology and culture, just as Victorians confused the physical and cultural when generalizing about the world's races (Bolt 1971; Alaya 1977; Rosenberg 1982). Activists did, of course, urge both the equality of the sexes and the differences between them. Pointing up the differences was, we have already argued, a shrewd tactic; one that acknowledged women's pride in being women and the greater responsiveness of men to demands based on women's special needs. The drawback was that if the two emphases were used simultaneously, feminists appeared inconsistent, and if one or the other was preferred, they could only advance some of their objectives and limited their appeal.

Given the size and variety of the female population, and the need to make practical progress in order to gain and retain credibility, it is hard to see how the feminists could have done much better. Had they been merely prudent, they would not have spoken out as adventurously as they did on the family and sexuality and would have avoided all inflated claims, particularly about the consequences of their enfranchisement. But reformers have generally needed to exaggerate to break down the apathy that normally supports the status quo, and in response to the exaggerated claims of their opponents. Had they been merely consistent, feminists would not have undermined their attack on separate spheres for the sexes as artificially created rather than natural, by accepting – either out of conviction or when it suited – the importance of women's natural attributes. However, modern historians of women, who have carefully distinguished between sexual differences in the biological sense and the cultural or gendered systems of inequality that have been built on these differences, recognize that gender history has provoked new contention.

It may indeed have stimulated scholars to look at women's experiences in a wider social context, recognizing the importance of other organizing variables in history (like class and race), breaking down divisions between the private and the public, and accepting that men and women alike live gendered lives. Yet in doing so it has challenged the preoccupation of women's history with the particularity of women's lives (Scott 1988), and practitioners of that history have been reluctant to abandon what they had to fight so hard to establish. After all, as late as the nineteenth century it was a commonplace that, far from having a distinct history, women had no history, had left no useful records, produced no great public figures, and influenced no great transforming forces or events (Douglas 1978). A further complication for current commentators on the emergence of feminist ideology is the application to history of post-structuralist theories, which reject the notion of natural categories and definitive texts, and present knowledge as constructed and partial. The past, by this interpretation, cannot be authoritatively interpreted, but historians can self-consciously seek to make their procedures less selective and devise a "discourse" based on sources of every kind (Rendall 1991, Stock-Morton 1991).

Applying the insights of post-structuralism to the debate about women's sexuality, position in society and case for the vote from the seventeenth to the nineteenth century, Denise Riley has illuminated the fluidity of the term "women": "historically, discursively constructed, and always relatively to other categories which themselves change". And she has shown how feminism has sought both to disengage from and lay claim to the category "women", torn between protesting "against over-feminisation and under-feminisation": between the pursuit of sexual equality and the celebration of female difference. Building a social movement around such an unstable category as "women" has required, in Riley's judgement, "the systematic fighting-out of that instability – which need not worry us" (Riley 1988; also Poovey 1988). And on the whole the differences between activists over how to project women's cause did not encumber them unduly until the interwar years of the twentieth century. Then, having achieved some of their early goals and lost some of their early momentum, feminists were compelled to reassess their philosophy, and found it more than usually testing to appeal to women as a collective. Although the women's movements did not therefore cease to exist, it was very tempting to give undue attention to single issue campaigns while so much remained to be done and so many critics were ready to pronounce feminism redundant. In this unfriendly climate it did not help that the feminists' message was reaching fewer people, proportionately, than it had done at the time of the First World War. Despite the fact that the women's movements attracted some of the best educated and most original activists of their time, no reform publications can hope to compete with the combined strength of the pamphlets, books, journals and newspapers that, whether deliberately or casually, uphold the status quo. This disparity was especially evident by the 1920s, when the financial resources of feminism were strained and the expansion of general periodicals for women, sensitive to social trends and the requirements of their advertisers, only enhanced the traditional image of female domesticity (Chafe 1972; Lemons 1973; Pugh 1992).

CHAPTER TWO

The shaping influence of class and race

We have seen how feminists spoke and wrote about the universality of sisterhood at the outset of their movement. But just as ideological differences became clearer with the passage of time, so too did the differences among women that related to class and race. The feminist campaign in both countries for most of the nineteenth century was dominated by middle-class women, allowing opponents to say that its activists were unrepresentative; and to follow on with the charge that the feminists' programme contained little of value for their working-class sisters. Even a feminist writer like Mabel Atkinson declared in 1913 that "among the working women there is less sex consciousness" (quoted in Alexander 1988). It is true that mobilizing a cross-section of women was extraordinarily hard, since those outside the middle class might either scorn or have no leisure for feminism; while those willing to act might find the opportunity to improve their circumstances through family and community activities, or through class and racial groups, all in the company of men from their own background. On the other hand, most reform and political movements of the period relied on the middle class, because its members had obvious advantages that they could put to use: namely money, time, social confidence and connections, education, a sense of obligation to those less fortunate, and smaller families to require their attention. In addition, many feminists felt a keen resentment that middle-class men were deriving more than they were from the century's changes and opportunities (Banks 1986; Buechler 1990).

The willingness to acknowledge the implications of class for their endeavours was stronger among English feminists than their trans-atlantic counterparts. Having secured independence by 1783, Americans had committed themselves to a new society based on respect for individual rights. The Constitution affected individuals, ignored classes and repudiated hereditary privilege. Education, the riches of a vast continent, limited government and equality of opportunity would theoretically give people of all kinds the ability to rise. The practice was different. In the first half of the nineteenth century the United States witnessed the strengthening of slavery in the southern states, discrimination against free blacks, dispossession of the Indians, mass immigration that aggravated existing urban and poverty problems, more assertive government, and increasingly vociferous complaints from the labouring classes. As ready as Victorians to confront the concept of race and unite whites behind a mission to "civilize" the "inferior" races, Americans were too anxious about the erosion of their vaunted exceptionalism and about the straining bonds of union to reconcile themselves to class divisions on the British pattern (Pole 1978; Horsman 1981). They remained determined to avoid them in their public rhetoric, and to prevent them from becoming a factor around which political parties were organized or legislation was promoted. The result was an awkwardness between American women drawn from different social levels, at least during the nineteenth century (Janiewski 1985; Stansell 1986; Ginzberg 1990).

In Britain, by contrast, the centrality of class could not be denied. The ruling elite was not destroyed by external crises and pressures from below during the late eighteenth and early nineteenth century: rather, it recovered and increased its authority (Colley 1992). A self-conscious and expansive middle class contended with this elite for power, and a diverse working class struggled for improvement through political organization and economic protest, as Britain felt the impact of the industrial revolution decades before the United States. British commentators might be worried about class questions, including aristocratic excesses and working-class threats, yet they did not deny their importance. As early as the 1850s, English feminists were ready to act on this perception.

They were then prompted to do so by an awareness that women outnumbered men by over half a million, and that working-class women and poor women of the middle class were particularly vulnerable. Working-class women suffered because employers welcomed them into the paid workforce in the expectation that they would be cheap and pliable employees. Poorer middle-class women suffered because their gentility required them to sustain a certain style of life, commonly as governesses, and hence prevented them from competing with working-class women for factory jobs. These paid better than the occupation of governess that, as novelists and moralists alike had observed, was overcrowded and could be wearisome and socially dispiriting. What was worse, since the often ill-educated and aspiring governess was lodged in the heart of the bourgeois family, she might do untold harm to the ideal of domesticity if carelessly chosen (Hammerton 1979; Peterson 1980; Poovey 1988; Renton 1991).

From the 1850s, English feminists undoubtedly looked to the interests of middle-class women by pressing for higher education, entry to the professions, and the vote on the same terms as men, that is for women of property. But they simultaneously tried to provide practical help for female job seekers, and to assist women's emigration to the colonies. From the 1870s onwards, they were organizing female unions and involving women in the co-operative movement. They also sought to modify the opposition of male unionists to collaborating with women at a time when employers opposed labour solidarity, women lacked experience and numbers in the paid workforce, and it was feared that the industrialization process would, by taking more women out of the domestic economy, jeopardize their health, expose them to moral temptation, erode community disciplines, weaken the family and depress men's wages. Although radical suffragists in the United States had in the late 1860s briefly attempted to secure female allies in the labour movement, the attempt had failed due to a similar combination of factors, compounded by the national aversion to campaigns built upon class. American feminists did not seriously resume such efforts until towards the end of the nineteenth century. They generally looked to manage rather than confront group differences in the tense climate created by the triumph of capitalism and Darwinist justifications of inequality (DuBois 1978; Tax 1979; Buhle 1981; Ginzberg 1990). And many would have agreed with one of their leading suffragists, Carrie Chapman Catt, that for a long time working women were "indifferent" to the vote (*Jus Suffragii* 1907).

By the twentieth century, however, feminists in both countries were involved in helping working women to unionize and agitate for better conditions, and other aspects of their programmes were clearly directed at this constituency. Clubs and settlement houses were established that provided practical help and social amenities for urban slum dwellers. Efforts were made to bring labouring women into suffragism, and the drive to reform the marriage laws had, as intended, eventually aided them by securing female control over earnings as well as property, making divorce more easily obtainable in America, and facilitating separations and maintenance orders in England. Rather more contentious, but no less indicative of the willingness of prosperous women to consider the difficulties of their poorer sisters, were the campaigns to assist prostitutes while curtailing prostitution; to improve the home making and health of working-class women; and generally to produce welfare measures for women that acknowledged their special needs. In Victorian fiction, too, pure women were frequently depicted as befriending fallen women, just as they did in life and with a comparable risk of breaking down the approved distance between the classes (Coslett 1988).

There are a number of problems associated with this social reform wing of feminism, whose adherents have been variously described as social feminists, maternalist feminists and welfare feminists (O'Neill 1969b; Pugh 1992; Koven & Michel 1993). Its impact is hard to assess independently from that of other reformers engaged in similar ventures. Its campaigns improved the lives of women (and children) without transforming the status quo. And its activists might be faulted for exploiting their power and for unattractive attitudes towards those they were committed to helping. Poor women were often seen as victims to be pitied, or as degraded individuals in need of improvement and control. They for their part might be resentful of patronage, uneasily aware of differences of outlook, irked by their disadvantages, and restlessly conscious that in the public arena they had few opportunities for independent action (O'Neill 1969b; Jacoby 1975; Liddington & Norris 1978; Summers 1979; Dye 1980; Chinn 1988; Lewis 1991a).

We should not therefore exaggerate the gulf between women – the touchiness on the one side, the arrogance on the other. Even before the rise of mass culture in the 1920s, technological developments and the forces of advertising had helped to democratize clothing considerably on each side of the Atlantic. Women from different classes looked more alike than they had done in previous eras, and had more contact as literacy, transport and communications improved. Welfare legislation and practical assistance were frequently welcomed by working women, if censorious home visits and lectures on morality were not (Peiss 1986). The poor and the prosperous needed to learn from one another, and to build alliances. And with difficulty, they did.

Despite the irritation felt by labour organizers like the American garment worker Pauline Newman over the "privileged few . . . speaking for and ruling the mass" (Pauline Newman Papers), there were middle-class feminists and an influential element from the upper class who determinedly reached out across the class divide. Notable in England were the university educated activist in urban improvement and suffragism, Esther Roper; the Irish-born poet who worked for the suffrage movement, Eva Gore-Booth; the organizer of working women in the East End of London, Sylvia Pankhurst; the campaigners for female unionization, Lady Emilia Dilke and Clementina Black; and the leader of the progressive wing of the women's temperance campaign in the 1890s, Lady Henry Somerset. In the United States, they included Margaret Dreier Robins of the Women's Trade Union League (1903); Vida Scudder and Jane Addams, the influential writers and settlement house residents; Florence Kelley, the crusading reformer and socialist author; Frances Willard, the charismatic head of the women's temperance crusade in its most successful phase; and Harriot Stanton Blatch, daughter of Mrs Stanton and galvanizer of suffragism in New York State.

By the First World War, the number of working-class women prominent in the British feminist movement had increased considerably, in recognition of the fact that the cause and those it involved had something to offer. After studying a sample of 98 feminist leaders, Banks (1986) found that in the cohorts born between 1849 and 1871, and 1872 and 1891, working women began to approach a quarter of the total. The American situation was very similar. Native-born working women and immigrant women, who might once have had little time and received little encouragement for activism outside their immediate groups, were making their presence felt in suffrage, trade union, club and community endeavours (Yans-McLaughlin 1977; Tax 1979; Dye 1980; Eisenstein 1983; DuBois 1987; Scott

1991). Unfortunately, this development was counterbalanced in England from the 1870s by an irrepressible dispute about the validity of protective industrial legislation, and in the early twentieth century the quarrel spread to the United States.

Legislation to control women's hours and conditions at work emerged first among English feminists because their country had experienced the disadvantages of industrialization before America did and because the British parliamentary system made it easier to secure such laws than it was in the United States. There, if the federal political structure allowed state experimentation with welfare legislation and variation in the laws enacted, the Constitution limited interference in workers' liberty of contract and, as we have noted, opposition to class legislation was entrenched. The debate over protection consequently became more heated and disruptive in American feminist circles, with those of an individualistic outlook convinced that "What women need is power, not protection. We must gain power, so that we can be free to develop the best that is in us" (*Equal rights* 1923). The weakness of trade unionism also played a part in the United States, where activists, admitting that women union members were "an ever-changing, shifting group" (WTUL of America Papers), were more tempted than they were in England to see legislative safeguards as an alternative, rather than a supplement, to labour organization.

As the matter was contested in England, however, it was quite worrying enough, since it entailed the open airing of class questions, revealed a generational gulf between the feminist protagonists, and divided both middle-class feminists and women workers. Pioneer English feminists, influenced by liberal ideas about personal freedom and competition in the economy, attacked protective laws that applied only to women. They saw them as a denial of their adult status, and likely to be abused by hostile male unionists to deny women jobs or reduce their earnings, thereby buttressing the domestic ideology and separate spheres for the sexes. Feminist leaders tended to differ about who best understood the needs of working women, and on the larger significance of regulation. Labouring women appear to have been divided specifically about whether legislation would help or hinder them at work. In the judgement of historians, the results were mixed, gains being made by children and male and female factory operatives but not the sweatshop workers, whose wages might plummet even further. Younger feminists, often influenced by detailed social surveys of working conditions, inclined to the view of the social activist, Beatrice Webb, that "law . . . is the mother of freedom" (quoted in Alexander 1988). When they did not patronize them as outdated, they accused their opponents of following the prejudices of their class: of assuming that because they needed an end to legislative restrictions in order to enter the professions, freedom from restrictions was equally appropriate for poorer women. Both sides in the debate made telling points. For example, while the unions did, indeed, support protection with a view to using it to their advantage, it was sensible to seek an alliance with them, since feminists were not in a position to organize unions and collective action by women workers on a large scale. Yet the participants were not inclined to be charitable towards each other in either country, and their differences could be cited unhelpfully by the critics of feminism (Soldon 1978; Strachey 1978; Becker 1981; Kessler-Harris 1982; Steinberg 1982; Sklar 1985; Rubinstein 1986; Cott 1987; Lehrer 1987; Levine 1987; Goldin 1988; Caine 1992; Skocpol 1995).

Among those critics were socialists, in Britain and the United States alike, but neither socialism as an ideology nor parties of the left were able to offer a secure base for feminists, though laying claim to the loyalty of women from the working class. Prospects for such a base were not improved by the habit of many bourgeois feminists, until the 1920s, of regarding feminism as above party politics: a common reformer stance. Any attempt to marry feminism and socialism was bound to be difficult because although each developed over time, the variant most significant when feminism was strong – that is Marxism – was the least helpful to women. Whereas utopian socialism had aimed at equality and freedom in all aspects of society, the contrast between feminism and Marxism was stark. Both were concerned with power, inequality and social change; yet while feminists stressed the divisive and dominant impact of sexuality on women, men and society, socialists emphasized the importance of production, the uniqueness of its capitalist mode, the creation of class divisions, and the historical necessity of beginning human emancipation with a particular class: the proletariat. It was possible for socialists to recognize the exploitation of women within the family, once it became divorced from production. It was possible for them to expose capitalism's desire to have a female reserve army of labour and a bloc of female consumers. It was not possible for feminists to ignore men's domination of the socialist movement, or to accept their elevation of natural differences between the sexes as justifying the ideal of a family wage earned by men on behalf of all family members. Equally problematical was the impatience of male radicals with women's complicating feelings and demands, especially when those demands were for individual rights or expressed by a privileged minority on behalf of the entire female sex (Engels 1966; Banks 1981; Mackinnon 1982; Taylor 1983; Lewis 1984; Scott 1988; Guarneri 1991). Under the circumstances, it is not surprising that before the twentieth century working-class women found it more difficult to assert themselves in the parties of the left than to join the independent cross-class campaigns organized by feminists for unionization and the vote.

The American socialist movement made slow progress among women from the 1870s in the face of the national aversion to class politics, the conservatism of male socialists about female roles, and the foreign flavour it acquired due to the dominant influence of German immigrants. But from the end of the nineteenth century to the First World War, a period of political ferment, support for socialism grew. Women founded independent socialist clubs and socialists attempted to recruit women, as well as giving more backing to their concerns, including suffrage, birth control and industrial action. Mainstream politicians took the potential of socialism seriously and socialists themselves would never again make such encouraging gains (Tax 1979; Buhle 1981). By contrast, the immediate post-war years saw the resurgence of political conservatism, in reaction to the establishment of the American Communist Party, labour militancy, the migration northwards of southern blacks, and record levels of immigration. When good times returned in 1923, organized labour found it hard to advance in the still stagnant old industries, while employers in the buoyant sector of the economy offered their workers benefits that further undermined the attractions of both the unions and socialism.

A new opportunity for labour and the left did appear to come during the 1930s, with the Depression and the ensuing New Deal policies of the Democratic president, Franklin Delano Roosevelt. The economic collapse was particularly severe and protracted in the United States, contrasting horribly with the prosperity that had

preceded it, undermining faith in *laissez-faire* liberalism and creating unusual sympathy for radical activists and their proposals. For a time, the Communist Party was willing to collaborate with the liberal groups that were fighting fascism, involving itself with their efforts to secure women's civil and political rights. It also backed female unionization drives and strike action, and published literature directed to women's interests. As a result, women constituted between 30 and 40 per cent of the party's membership in the 1930s. Yet there were never many female leaders in the communist movement and women complained that their male comrades frequently endorsed the conventional division of labour in the family, and valued them only in supportive, backroom and social roles (Dennis 1977; Ware 1982). Feminists were simply not in a strong enough position to persuade the key shapers of the Communist Party to share their views on sexual oppression.

In Britain, by the last two decades of the nineteenth century, women discontented with the achievements of liberal individualism could look for an alternative to an array of small socialist groups, and were particularly attracted to the Fabians, whose youthful and highly intellectual adherents downplayed the class struggle and attached more importance to statistical inquiry, state intervention and the achievement of a broad collectivism. Women comprised a third to a half of the Fabian membership, and formed their own, primarily middle-class, Fabian Women's Group in 1908, which had an enrolment of around 230 after four years. This somewhat austere alliance of writers, lecturers, teachers, medical, public service and trade union personnel set out to reconcile socialism and feminism. Recognizing the class divisions between women, its supporters none the less focused on women's common concerns. Their publications meticulously investigated the economic conditions that led to female dependency. They aimed to educate working women on the social questions that vitally affected them, and argued that female emancipation could be achieved by means of a just rate of pay for women working outside the home and mothers' pensions for those working within the family (Alexander 1988; Dyhouse 1989).

These and other left-wing British women had the additional option of joining the Independent Labour Party after 1893, the Labour Party after 1906 and the Communist Party after the First World War. Although the small ILP and CP welcomed such women as activists, they were not prepared to give them power. But the rise of a mass Labour Party, which achieved office in 1924 and 1929–31, seemed to offer opportunities to English feminists that their American sisters did not enjoy. The suffrage campaigners had seen the need of cultivating links with Labour once their courtship of the Liberals had plainly proved a disappointment, and in 1912 the Labour Party had committed itself to opposing any suffrage bill that did not include women. What is more, the party's support for legislation to protect women in industry and in their roles as wives and mothers found favour with many working-class women as well as some of their middle-class allies. On the other hand, protective laws were partly designed to buttress men's supremacy, local branches were not necessarily as sympathetic to women's demands as national leaders, female membership declined during the difficult Depression years, and there was a split within Labour ranks between women who put the party line first and a losing minority who gave priority to feminist considerations (Liddington & Norris 1978; Rowan 1982; Collette 1989; Pugh 1992).

While feminists were more assertive in the Labour than the Conservative Party, it did not help that Labour was still fairly inexperienced at the national level and dependent on Liberal support through the 1920s. Male leaders had no intention of doing more for working women than was necessary to secure their votes, and could point to the fight against unemployment and fascism as Labour's proper preoccupation. Pressure upon them was reduced when Labour women became isolated from former feminist friends, who were disenchanted with the party's policies. Accordingly, Labour did little to promote women candidates for promising constituencies, to encourage women's progress up the party hierarchy, or to challenge conventional prejudices on controversial issues, notably birth control, family allowances and equal pay for the sexes (Banks 1981; Smith 1984; Harrison 1989; Thane 1990; Pugh 1992; Graves 1994).

Officials of the Women's Trade Union League of America noted in 1926 that "For . . . millions of women, group conditions must be treated by group action, and the labor woman therefore has a collective ideal, with a program which may sometimes restrict individual liberty in the interests of the group" (WTUL of America Papers). All too often, however, their group interests were neglected on each side of the Atlantic. Yet giving priority to the group meant that women's

individual rights were harder to secure. Effective women's movements required organizations and activists concerned with both; and
while they produced them, the tension between the two was never
resolved.

Distinctions based on race posed even more dangers for feminists,
though they might at times ignore them, just as privileged women
claiming to speak for all women might choose to ignore their own
advantageous class position. They were of most immediate importance in the United States, where race consciousness was kept high by
the aftermath of slave emancipation (1865), the need to make peace
with the Indians, and the increase of immigrants from southern and
eastern Europe, who were alleged to be inferior to their north European predecessors. White women were among those who responded
with genuine humanitarianism to these challenges. They provided
funds and teachers for the schools set up to meet the demand for
education from the ex-slaves in the South, and they joined other self-
styled "friends of the Indian" in pressing for the reform of American
Indian policy (Bolt 1987). The Women's National Indian Association, formed in Philadelphia in 1879, made "the elevation of Indian
women and homes" its particular preserve, and claimed to have
recruited to the organization "some of the best women of the land,
among whom are those well known in the religious, literary, scientific, and social world". According to the Association's president,
speaking in 1885, its existence was "due to that enlightened spirit of
philanthropy which, as a natural outgrowth of Christian principle,
permeates as never before the womanhood of the land. It is this spirit
that is making woman a most potent adjunct in the solving of the
social problems that press upon the enlightened conscience in this
day of grand endeavors for uplifting of the race." In supporting
Indian education, missionary work, improvements in the Indian
service and the guaranteeing of Indian legal rights, the women condemned the prejudices of their time without entirely escaping them:
as one activist put it, the Indians, "Though savages . . . are not children" (*Annual report* of the WNIA for 1884; *Address of the president
of the women's national Indian association*, 1875; *Indians and their
helpers*, n.d.).

Such "friends of the Indian" are entitled to be described as social
feminists in their determination to give practical help to women,
whom they regarded as more amenable to change than men and

35

more influential because of their responsibility for rearing the next generation. Their objectives gave them something in common with the female settlement house residents who, from the 1890s, were engaged with the immigrant poor and likewise gave special attention to women and children. But whereas the generally well placed settlement house women attempted to break down class antipathies by living and working with the slum dwellers, the members of the Woman's National Indian Association mostly exercised their goodwill at a distance from the Indians. In the case of African-American women, by the later nineteenth century white feminists were still further removed from the close contacts that can dissipate racial misconceptions.

The distancing of white American feminists from their black sisters has been strongly criticized, and presented as the direct result of white prejudice and calculation (Davis 1981; hooks 1981; Terborg-Penn 1983; Giddings 1987). Although such criticisms have real force, the way in which that distancing process evolved needs to be examined. American feminism was not constructed on abolitionist foundations alone, but also owed much to women's urban reform activities and religious endeavours that were not noted for their radicalism on social questions. In working through separate auxiliaries in the anti-slavery movement, white women were yielding to men's pressures. In compelling black female abolitionists to do the same, they showed themselves equally incapable of rising above contemporary fears about the consequences of mixing up the races and sexes. Given the violence shown to anti-slavery advocates and the alarm aroused by the charge that they favoured racial interbreeding, it is heartening to find that there were a handful of black women abolitionists who experienced kindness and comradeship from their white counterparts while pursuing their complicated fight against slavery, race prejudice and female subordination (Yellin 1989; Yee 1992; Bolt 1993).

Black female activists certainly could not be held responsible for the failure of the feminist campaign to secure the vote by the Fourteenth and Fifteenth Amendments to the Constitution (1868 and 1870), during the Reconstruction period following the Civil War. They played only a small part in that campaign (DuBois 1978), and they, too, were excluded from the franchise. Yet it was understandable that some white women activists, having been deserted in the amendment struggle by white and black male abolitionists, turned away from old connections. They preferred, instead, to build up independent suffrage societies, focusing on the promising western territories and states, and seeking a women's suffrage amendment to the Constitution. The southern states were neglected for compelling reasons. Abolitionism had been driven out of the South before the Civil War, and having little common ground and little alternative, black and white women looked for support to their own communities rather than each other (Lebsock 1984; White 1985; Fox-Genovese 1988). Reconstruction encouraged the further separation of the races, something that ex-slaves understandably favoured, as did their former owners. Southern conservatives had engineered the end of Reconstruction by 1877, skilfully appealing to Americans' respect for state rights, and from then on through the 1880s, the South sustained its own charitable and reform interests. These did not include interracial ventures or suffragism, which was unfavourably associated with the weakening of the family and the modernizing spirit of the North. By the 1890s, black and white southern women were active in racially separate clubs, church and temperance societies, trying to improve their localities, protect children, sustain missionary work, and enhance their economic and social circumstances (Scott 1970, 1991; Loewenberg & Bogin 1976; Hine 1981; Sterling 1984). It was not until this decade, against a background of economic distress and political turbulence, that women's suffrage groups appeared.

Black women drawn to such social activism struggled with formidable disadvantages. Frequently very poor, they had limited prospects of acquiring higher education or breaking out of low paid, menial jobs. When country dwellers moved west, or into urban areas in search of less constricting lives, they achieved economic and social gains at the expense of family solidarity (Jones 1985). To compound their difficulties, many whites had convinced themselves that women of colour were more sexually accommodating than white women (Giddings 1984). Such a belief sprang from the contemporary association of "lower" races with the natural expression of feelings and behaviour frowned upon in "civilized" societies. It was strengthened by the argument that when racial mixing occurred between blacks and whites, only the African-American woman was involved. White racists denied the possibility of white women being attracted to black men, and made critical comments on the black family without acknowledging the social conditions that forced more black than white women into the paid workforce (Bederman 1995).

Black feminists none the less emerged in both the South and the North. Among their number were the author and lecturer Frances Harper; the teacher and suffragist Mary Church Terrell; the crusading journalist Ida B. Wells; the editor and suffragist Josephine Ruffin; the doctors Rebecca Cole and Susan Smith McKenney Steward; the teacher and writer Anna Julia Cooper; and the banker and activist in innumerable organizations for racial, female and community advancement Maggie Lena Walker. All of these women, contrary to stereotype, were eminently respectable in appearance and behaviour, and some of them joined with white feminists in club and suffrage gatherings, and in the meetings of the Association for the Advancement of Women (1873–97). Co-operation was facilitated by the similar class background of the two groups of activists and by the small number of black feminists involved. Acceptance in the African-American community was facilitated by activists showing themselves sensitive to the status anxieties of black men and stressing the importance of racial self help as much as the rights of women, presenting the two issues as intertwined.

The campaign of Ida Wells against lynching in the South is a good example of how a practice ostensibly directed against African-American men for alleged offences against white women was properly interpreted by a female black activist as a woman's issue – part of a general effort "to 'keep the nigger down'", and to deny the existence of cohabitation between white women and black men (Wells 1970). Of similar relevance to black women were discrimination in employment and public facilities, and the denial of the vote to either black women or black men (in defiance of the Reconstruction amendments). However, the connection of sexual and racial oppression has not been widely accepted by whites, who have tended to see women of colour as being engrossed in their various racial movements. In reaction, there has been some recent black support for the word "womanism", to distinguish a philosophy committed to sexual and racial equality (Brown 1990).

Despite its tolerably cordial beginnings, the relationship between black and white feminists deteriorated towards the end of the nineteenth century as the segregation of the races became more severe, especially in the South. Bowing to local prejudices, the General Federation of Women's Clubs (1890) declined to admit black clubs and the normally intrepid Frances Willard accepted the exclusion of black women from the southern Woman's Christian Temperance Union. Her organization, declared Willard, stood "not only for total abstinence and prohibition, but for no sectarianism in religion, no sectionalism in politics, no sex in citizenship. We recognize State rights as to the adoption of these principles" (WCTU national pamphlet). Although the Union proselytized among African-Americans, Willard did not see the need to add opposition to racial discrimination to its principles, and was willing to allow the southern states to determine their members and programme in all respects. Anxious to foster the suffrage efforts of southern white women, the National American Woman's Suffrage Association took the same line after 1903. In doing so, it knew that many southern white men and a number of white women favoured the exclusion of all blacks from the ballot and the enfranchisement of white women to strengthen white supremacy. The Association's excuse was that any women voters would be worth having – a stance that did not seem too much of a betrayal of feminism in an organization that also contained advocates of an educational qualification for the suffrage to uphold the ascendancy of America's core "Anglo-Saxon" population (Wheeler 1993).

Black feminists were quick to acknowledge any help they received from whites and to urge that "women should stand together for the womanhood of the world" (Scott 1991); but they were increasingly forced back on their own separate organizations for the rest of our period. These existed at the local, state and national level, where bodies like the National Association of Colored Women, the National Association of Wage Earners and the International Council of Women of the Darker Races supplemented the work done by African-American women and men in the Urban League and the National Association for the Advancement of Colored People. They were notable for their freedom from the constricting cult of "true womanhood"; for their emphasis upon the importance of motherhood, paid work and equal rights; and for their acceptance of suffragism in the North and the need for non-political operations in the South (Boris 1993). Middle-class activists remained dominant outside the community groups, and relations with white women continued to be problematic. Hence, during the 1920s, if southern feminists at last engaged in interracial endeavours, including an anti-lynching drive, black women in the South who sought help in registering to vote from the feminists of the National Woman's Party were refused assistance, on the grounds that it was a racial matter. In an era when feminist associations of all kinds found it hard to retain members and funds, the frequent aloofness of white feminists compounded the difficulties of their black counterparts, encouraging them to look to black men for help (Lerner 1972; Hall 1979; Hull et al. 1982; Terborg-Penn 1983; Cott 1987; Neverdon-Morton 1989; Thomas 1992; Higginbotham 1993; Hine 1995; Salem 1990).

During the 1930s, black activists did receive aid from an unusually influential white woman: the president's wife, Eleanor Roosevelt. A humanitarian and activist interested in black and female concerns, Mrs Roosevelt disguised her radicalism with a cloak of ladylike dignity, rather as the iconoclastic Elizabeth Stanton had done decades earlier (Lasch 1971; Ware 1981; Griffith 1984; Cook 1992). But as before, black women had to rely mainly on their own networks, and their lobbying power was helpfully consolidated in 1935 when the National Council of Negro Women was founded by the black New Dealer, Mary McLeod Bethune. The Council represented nearly 850,000 women, and worked for their participation in "civic, political, economic, and educational activities and institutions". Black Americans of both sexes benefited from the New Deal welfare measures and more public appointments than they had enjoyed under any other president. In the end, however, all minority groups were disappointed with the half measures of an administration that was committed to liberal, not radical change. And the persistently high level of unemployment throughout the decade had its most devastating effect on the already vulnerable black population (Holt 1964; Weiss 1983; Fitzgerald 1985).

The emphasis so far has been on the endeavours of African-American women, because they belonged to the largest non-white minority group in the United States and had been bound up with feminism from its beginnings. Yet Native American women activists emerged early, not least out of the otherwise unsuccessful pan-Indian, off-reservation boarding schools supported by the government from the 1870s. They attended meetings of the "friends of the Indian" and of the Society of American Indians (1911), though few became officers in the SAI. And by the 1920s they had formed the National Society of Indian Women, encouraged by the National Federation of Women's Clubs that, in its interest in Native Americans' welfare, somewhat compensated for its unwelcoming attitude towards black club women (Bolt 1987).

For American women of Hispanic and Asian descent, a relationship with white feminism was impossible before the second half of the twentieth century. Their tradition of activism had matured only by the 1960s, and was constrained by poverty, racial discrimination, family responsibilities, and conservative male attitudes towards wives and daughters. It none the less grew at the community level, with the emphasis on self help and association in women's clubs; and led very slowly to involvement in protest organizations that pressed for education, economic and political rights. Changes for these women might be brought about by developments in the United States, such as growing opportunities for working outside the home, unionization possibilities, missionary and reformer efforts to make them acculturate, and the Depression of the 1930s. They were also influenced by events in their countries of origin, with which ties were not easily severed (Sánchez 1994; Yung 1994).

British women of colour had even less prospect of establishing links with feminists before the 1960s, when their numbers had been greatly augmented by immigrants from the Commonwealth. They were a tiny fraction of the total population throughout our period, since the small community of Chinese, Indian and black Britons was primarily male. Comprising mainly soldiers, seamen and the descendants of slaves, persons of colour were concentrated in the cities, particularly London. Their limited numbers and frequent poverty tended to make them invisible to the prosperous, and they did not provoke race riots or legal discrimination on the American pattern. Moreover racial mixing had taken place, with white women helping to integrate the newcomers into a country notable for its ethnocentrism. But British racial attitudes hardened in the course of the nineteenth century as a result of the decline of the anti-slavery movement, augmented Irish and Jewish immigration, imperial crises, a heightened awareness of class and national identity, and the dissemination of new scientific ideas on race (Bolt 1971, 1984). Where once the imperial dignitaries, students, black minstrels, American Indians, and black abolitionists from the United States had been

41

cordially received if their rank warranted it, racial prejudice increasingly shaped the response to non-white visitors and residents alike (Lorimer 1978).

The anti-slavery movement did, however, bring British women into contact with imperial issues and with the problems of women of colour, and they gave a warm welcome to the black abolitionists Ellen Craft and Sarah Remond, who for a time worked in Britain (Ripley 1985; Midgley 1992). As late as the 1890s, when Ida Wells took her campaign against lynching across the Atlantic, she too encountered interest and kindness, noting her fruitful contacts with Isabella Mayo, a Scottish writer who offered practical help to East Indian victims of the caste system, and Catherine Impey, an English Quaker and "the editor of *Anti-Caste*, a magazine published in England on behalf of the natives of India . . . [who] was . . . interested in the treatment of darker races everywhere". Yet such visitors experienced irritants as well as plaudits, and their reception may have been coloured by British pleasure in being ahead of the United States in well doing. According to Sir Edward Russell, writing during Wells's visit of 1894, "It is an essential part of the business of great nations to shame each other" (Wells 1970); and acting on this assumption, the British also liked to point out that their management of Indian affairs in Canada was superior to American conduct of Indian policy (Bolt 1987). In fact, by the 1870s anti-slavery endeavours no longer had their old importance for British women activists, some of whom were occupied with other causes and looked with a new degree of self interest at the challenges and opportunities afforded by the Empire.

Given the so-called surplus of women in Britain, the colonies were understandably seen as providing "honourable and profitable activity" for them as servants, missionaries, teachers, medical personnel, even adventurers (*Englishwoman's Journal*, 1872, XI; Trollope 1994). Women who were restless and delicate at home might become intrepid travellers when released from the constraints of conventional female behaviour. While much of the literature of empire was composed by men with boys and men in mind, women might also welcome the opportunity to find unusual tests beyond the reach of civilization. Conversely, a more numerous category of women set out to civilize the native woman, just as reformers aimed to uplift British working-class women. American women did not have similar opportunities, because the United States experienced only a brief period of colonial acquisition, at the end of the nineteenth century, before reverting to its normal economic means of asserting power abroad; and because it did not send out large numbers of settlers to the colonies it had acquired. Even so, there was considerable female interest in American imperialism and anti-imperialism alike, as well as support for and participation in missionary, anti-opium and social purity work abroad, sometimes in co-operation with the British (Willard 1894; Hunter 1984). In both the United States and Britain, and especially by the end of the nineteenth century, Darwinism and imperialism inclined some white women to regard themselves as the vanguards of a higher, Anglo-Saxon race. This kind of thinking was encouraged by eugenicists and politicians worried by a decline in the middle-class birthrate, and it might be strengthened when women wrote about or went to the colonies, where the female population was generally thought to be worse off than it was in British and American polite society.

In England, one of the earliest expressions of feminine concern about colonial women made outside the anti-slavery movement came as a result of the campaign to repeal the Contagious Diseases Acts of the 1860s. The legislation was designed to regulate prostitutes in naval and garrison towns, essentially to protect their patrons, and was opposed by feminists and social purists as an ill-judged assertion of male power and the double standard of morality. Subsequent attempts to sustain a comparable system in India, though securing some female backing on health grounds, met with strong objections from women who, like the leading anti-regulationist, Josephine Butler, saw their civilizing mission as extending to the Empire. And if Butler had no direct involvement with Indian women, there were British female activists – from the educationalist Mary Carpenter in the nineteenth century to the distinguished MP Eleanor Rathbone in the twentieth – whose concern was co-operative efforts to improve the education, welfare and organization skills of Indian women. By the 1930s, feminists were also pressing for Indian women to receive the vote, which some did in 1935. Of course such activists were nationalists and imperialists. They accepted the existence of the Empire, frequently took pleasure in being part of it, and worked with its politicians and institutions. But the imperial and international roles of British and other white women have been recently reassessed and are clearly more complicated than was once supposed (Barr 1976; Ballhatchet 1980; Berridge & Edwards 1981; Callaway 1987; Harrison 1987; Lind 1988; Burton 1990; Ramusack 1990; Rubinstein 1991; Strobel 1991; Chaudhuri & Strobel 1992; Rupp 1994; Burton 1994).

On the one hand, English feminists declared an interest in women throughout the world, regardless of race, rank or religion, seeking to dispel "the ignorance very generally existing in England" about foreign parts (*Englishwoman's Review*, VI, 1871). Advocates of constructive change, they proudly reported on gains made by women in the colonies, notably their enfranchisement in New Zealand (1893) and Australia (1893–1909), where victory had come without any of "the evils so confidently predicted" (Fawcett 1912). They effectively resisted the anti-suffragist argument that female enfranchisement would weaken the standing of the Empire in colonial possessions where male dominance was unquestioned. In short, social feminism transcended national boundaries. On the other hand, activists were inclined to see overseas women of colour as "hopeless, helpless victims", and denounced a range of foreign customs that made them so, including female circumcision in Africa and, in India, plural wives, the mistreatment of widows, and the "horrid system of early marriages" (*Englishwoman's Review*, XIV, 1873; VIII, 1871). When offering or acting on these opinions, they risked reducing native women to abstractions but their humanitarianism must be acknowledged. They were emphatically not akin to those white female imperialists who, insecure about their own position far from home, gave offence by rigidly drawing the colour line and deploring everything they did not understand.

Africa was a particular challenge to women, since few had settled there before the 1890s to report on the continent from a feminine point of view. Yet Olive Schreiner's novel, *The story of an African farm* (1883), had inspired countless feminists not only by its indictment of the condition of women but also by its depiction of a racially complex society and a powerful natural environment (Showalter 1978; Flint 1993). The Anglo-Boer War of 1899–1902, which put the pro-Boer Schreiner under virtual house arrest, increased British women's interest in the region while revealing once more the divisions between them, just as the debate over Indian prostitution had done. Many of those who appeared at the scene of war were merely curious and fashionable nuisances, indifferent to the suffering of native women and generally unconcerned about gender issues. But a few activists did interest themselves in the women and children confined to the concentration camps for dependents of Boer soldiers, and a notable confrontation developed between Emily Hobhouse, a feminist reformer who became a fearless critic of the camps and a friend of Olive Schreiner, and Millicent Fawcett, the much better known suffragist leader. Being an anti-Boer imperialist as well as a feminist, Mrs Fawcett was pleased to head an all-female official review of the camps, determined to disarm the opponents of women's emancipation, and anxious to defend her country's reputation. The final report was therefore by no means a simple account of the sufferings of her sex, and contained criticisms of the Boer women's ignorance and superstition. Neither Fawcett nor Hobhouse investigated the black camps, although Hobhouse was uneasy about their conditions (Roberts 1991; Rubinstein 1991).

Once the conflict was over, British women encouraged female emigration to South Africa, to link "the old country and the new colony together", to bring about a better balance between the sexes, to provide opportunities for the migrants, and to help make the future of the region "an era of Civilisation, of Progress, and of Illumination, where Semi-barbarism, Retrogression, and Ignorance for years have reigned supreme" (*The Imperial Colonist* 1902). As with earlier attempts to promote the emigration of women, the process was presented as benefiting colony and colonizers alike. Yet as with those earlier attempts, the bias was towards assisting the better class of emigrant, despite the difficulty in finding "a sufficient number of women of the right kind" (South African Colonisation Society Reports 1908–9). In consequence, while emigration projects found favour with feminists and non-feminists, they remained of limited usefulness as a means of improving the circumstances of British women.

CHAPTER THREE

Organization and leadership

If women were not supposed to be intellectually adventurous, they generally received praise for their practicality. Rich women frequently supervised large houses, and involved themselves in important social and political duties connected with the family. Poor women had to manage children, home work, paid work and tight budgets, while their middle-class sisters juggled with family, religious and humanitarian activities. Women of all kinds, finding that others had first claims on their services, learned to make the most of the time they could call their own. Moreover, their involvement in reform activities had, by the middle of the nineteenth century, given them experience in conducting meetings, producing literature, raising money and reaching out to a constituency. In the judgement of the British feminist author and editor, Bessie Parkes, women's "capacities for government and organization are not doubted by any one who has taken pains to write or read history" (Parkes 1865).

We should not, therefore, assume that the transition from reformer to feminist was an easy one. Women activists initially had been welcomed in various causes because they were willing to take on the least glamorous work, leaving policy making and public duties to men (Prochaska 1980). They had gradually enlarged their roles, yet as late as the 1870s, English women were seldom heard on the public platform, particularly as representatives of a secular movement (Shiman 1992). Some two decades earlier, benefiting from their country's democratic ethos and more advanced educational provision, women activists in the United States had undermined complaints that female public speaking was indecorous and unwarranted. But they had not supported the move of reformers before the Civil War towards a more institutionalized and businesslike benevolence (Ginzberg 1990), preferring the old emphasis upon converting the virtuous individual to a moral cause. Hence the American women's movement until the close of the 1860s had relied on state and national conventions, with little permanent, co-ordinating organization. By that point, the English movement had failed to produce such regular gatherings. It depended instead on single issue committees to push for reforms in the marriage laws, education and suffrage, though these were supplemented by a London headquarters and a Society for the Promotion of the Employment of Women, which had branches in provincial cities as well as the metropolis.

At the end of the 1860s, however, the need for organizational progress was accepted. From then until the First World War progress was remarkable, though not strictly symmetrical, on both sides of the Atlantic. In each country, women took advantage of favourable social developments to launch new associational efforts that were increasingly national in scope. They had devised their main goals swiftly but it had not been at all clear in the 1850s which objectives would be advanced first and by what collective means: external factors were frequently crucial determinants. The first breakthrough was the creation of organizations to fight for the suffrage: the National Society for Women's Suffrage (1868) in Britain, and the National Woman Suffrage Association (NWSA, 1869) and American Woman Suffrage Association (1869) in the United States. Feminists acted here because they were aware that their early steps towards emancipation had been hampered by female disfranchisement. It was also realized that the debates of the 1860s about giving the suffrage to additional groups of men could be helpful to women's demands. The existence of two American groups claiming to represent the nation was necessitated by personal differences between leading suffragists and principled disagreements about whether suffragists should concern themselves with a wide range of additional issues, the adherents of NWSA believing that they should. All three organizations drew strength from their linked local associations, which were allowed considerable latitude, despite the strengthening of nationalism and central government power as the nineteenth century progressed. For activists in Britain, the independence of Scottish reformers and the distinctive preoccupations of the Irish and Welsh made such a policy desirable. The size, regional variety and federal political system of the United States rendered it still more appropriate for their American sisters.

Parallel with this mobilization of interest in the vote went the emergence of organizations devoted to moral questions, or social purity: a cause that, more than suffragism, emphasized women's special qualities and concerns, and reflected an increasingly secularized public anxiety about the moral and health implications of urbanization and industrialization. Britain took the lead here, with the Ladies National Association for the Repeal of the Contagious Diseases Acts (LNA, 1869). Its campaign was against the British parliament's regulation of prostitution during the 1860s, in response to military and medical pressures. And in order to make an impact on the legislature, LNA activists evolved a network of branches, reaching out to newly enfranchised working men and, to a lesser extent, working women (Walkowitz 1980). Women did not monopolize the social purity drive. The LNA had the backing of a men's organization dedicated to repeal, the sexes eventually collaborated in bodies like the National Vigilance Association (1885), and the LNA merged with its male equivalent in 1913 to constitute the Association for Social and Moral Hygiene. Americans' interest in social purity issues had developed in the 1830s as the problems of the Old World infiltrated the New. It had been rendered ineffectual by the 1860s, as war tore the country apart, and was revitalized in the 1870s by the much publicized stand of British women against the Contagious Diseases Acts. As a result, new social purity organizations were formed, ranging from the moral education societies of the 1870s to the American Purity Alliance of the 1890s, and gaining support from existing religious, reform and women's groups, most importantly the Woman's Christian Temperance Association (WCTU, 1874). Appealing to feminist and non-feminist women alike, the WCTU became the biggest recruiter of American women throughout the 1870s and 1880s, confirming the enduring importance of religious motivations among female reformers in the United States, notwithstanding the steady secularization of reform endeavours as a whole. The British Woman's Temperance Association (1876), the nation's largest female temperance organization and the main mobilizer of women during these decades, did not enlarge its range of interests until the 1890s, when it added the word National to its title (NBWTA) but lost some of its former adherents over the move. Britain's temperance women also owed more to external influences – namely temperance crusaders from the United States and British male campaigners against drink – than did their American counterparts. English feminists with radical views on moral issues were more likely to be captured by the exciting social purity campaign than they were by temperance.

In the educational arena, the early progress of American women meant that by 1882 they were able to sustain an Association of Collegiate Alumnae, concerned to encourage applicants for college and to put graduates in touch with each other, not least so that they could debate their employment prospects. The Women's Educational Union (1871), the major organization of English activists, felt obliged to concentrate on improving secondary schooling for girls and the training of teachers, and it survived for little more than a decade, thereafter leaving the field to female teacher associations. However, British feminists continued to be more organizationally inventive when it came to economic improvements in the position of women, involving themselves in various cross-class enterprises devoted to the co-operation, welfare and unionization of working women: the Women's Protective and Provident League (1874), which by 1891 had become the Women's Trade Union League; the National Union of Women Workers (1874); and the Women's Co-operative Guild (WCG, 1883). And from the 1890s to the First World War, both British and American women activists, like their male contemporaries, sought ways of adjusting reform and political institutions to the problems created by exploitative industrialization and congested cities. The need to do so seemed peculiarly urgent to reformers in the United States, whose first leaders had hoped to avoid such European dilemmas and whose city governments lagged far behind those of Britain in trying to humanize the face of capitalism.

Accordingly, American women energetically adopted the settlement house from England and extended the activities of their clubs, which had proliferated since the 1860s and far outnumbered and outperformed English women's clubs. In 1903 they founded the Women's Trade Union League, in direct emulation of the British League; and from 1890 they set up consumers' leagues, that were linked by a National Consumers' League in 1899. As the trade union leagues and WCG had already done, consumers' leagues reached out to working women: specifically by investigating employment conditions, supporting protective legislation, and generally galvanizing prosperous consumers to exert their influence on behalf of those less fortunate. American women's pressures were, in addition, vital in securing the establishment of a federal Children's Bureau (1912) and Women's Bureau (1920), agencies that could compile data and influence federal government policy. During the same period, the organizational efforts of British feminists were distinctive in two ways. First, they worked with non-feminists for the two main political parties, through the Conservatives' Primrose League (1883) and the Women's Liberal Federation (1886). Party loyalties being less strong in the American political system, there were no equivalent bodies to recruit their unpaid services until the interwar years of the twentieth century. But though party considerations were given priority in the League and Federation, both bodies politicized women, who then took the opportunity to press their own interests. Secondly, British activists launched new cross-class ventures with a political and social agenda that included women's suffrage, these being the Women's Industrial Council (1894), the Women's Labour League (1906) and the National Federation of Women Workers (1906). In addition, organized suffragism expanded dramatically on each side of the Atlantic, and while the two branches of the American campaign had united in 1890 under the title of the National American Woman Suffrage Association (NAWSA), splinter groups sprang up in the British and American suffrage movements alike as new methods were tried, new members recruited, and the final victory remained elusive.

As one would expect, the First World War put a strain on organized feminism on each side of the Atlantic, although Britain was involved in the conflict three years before the United States. Reformers of every kind were expected to subordinate their sectional objectives to the national emergency. None the less, women seized the opportunity to create new agencies through which female war and peace work might be channelled, and kept suffrage associations alive until the vote was secured at the end of the conflict for all American women, and (to avoid a female voting majority) for those over thirty years of age in Britain. During the next two decades, energized by the suffrage breakthrough, they devised new organizations and adapted old ones to respond to fresh challenges and familiar injustices. Thus settlement houses, clubs, consumer leagues and labour groups still called upon the services of women activists, but were supplemented by birth control leagues, an array of bodies representing particular groups of women or campaigning on single issues of importance, and broader ranging alliances such as the National Woman's Party (NWP 1916) and the League of Women Voters (LWV 1920) in the United States, and the National Union of Societies for Equal Citizenship (NUSEC 1919) and the Six Point Group (SPG 1921) in Britain. Despite their shared objectives, British and American feminists also continued to direct their organizations towards their own special problems. Hence pressure had to be sustained in Britain for full female suffrage, secured in 1928; while the more severe Depression in the United States during the 1930s gave women with a long apprenticeship in reform associations a unique opportunity to raise their status in the Democratic Party, and to influence its reformist legislation.

It should be clear from this brief review that the organized English and American women's movements were not simply suffrage campaigns but rather multi-cause movements, whose organizational range increased as women gained experience and favourable circumstances presented themselves. Both movements sustained single issue associations (such as the suffrage societies became); umbrella organizations (such as the social purity and main temperance operations, the LWV, NUSEC and SPG); and cross-class endeavours (such as the trade union leagues and the WCG). Every type of organization had some kind of drawback and no association enjoyed uninterrupted growth. The danger of single issue alliances was that their narrow focus weakened members' commitment to the overall aims of feminism and rendered them indistinguishable from other small pressure groups. The danger of the wide-ranging operations was that disagreements about priorities and the wisdom of certain linkages commonly developed within them, as happened, for example, in the American temperance movement over connections with the suffragists. Furthermore, large organizations have often attracted supporters merely because they are successful or fashionable: cases in point would be the temperance and suffrage societies. Equally, in any reform effort, long established associations have lost backing because they found it difficult to change quickly, especially if they had some successes to safeguard: settlement houses, women's clubs, consumer and trade union leagues, and social purity groups eventually fell into this category. Yet even the newly formed ventures of the 1920s found themselves struggling in the adverse economic circumstances of the 1930s.

The riskiest organizations for feminists were those (for instance associated with social purity) where they combined with non-feminist women and men. Although such bodies offered freedom from anti-feminist sniping, they were likely to inhibit the expression of a feminist viewpoint among members. Separate feminist institutions offered the opposite alternative. The case for and against them is fairly obvious. Unless women could run their own movement, they could hardly persuade sceptics of their fitness to run anything else, while all-female associations gave them a power base from which to exert leverage in the wider world without entirely overthrowing the notion of separate spheres for the sexes (Freedman 1979). Conversely, welcoming men into female groups could alter women's style and invite subordination to representatives of the dominant sex. At the very least it might encourage a combination of elite women and men, thereby undercutting women's efforts to construct cross-class female alliances. The argument against separation was that by the end of the nineteenth century men and women lived less distinctive lives then they had done, would have to co-operate for female emancipation to be realized, and would be less likely to perpetuate unhelpful misconceptions about each other if they did so sooner rather than later. Support for separate organizations was strongest in the United States, reflecting both the power of its ideology of domesticity and women's faith in their right to the freedom of assembly, that was rooted in the Constitution and opportunely confirmed by their experiences in the anti-slavery struggle.

Like all reformers, feminists only managed to mobilize a fraction of their targeted constituency at any time, but did well enough from the 1890s through to the 1920s to undermine opponents' claims that they represented only an eccentric handful of women. In 1892, the WCTU claimed some 50,000 members, and eight years later the NBWTA claimed around 10,000. In 1910, the General Federation of Women's Clubs spoke for 800,000 women. By the First World War, NAWSA's membership was estimated at 200,000, that of Britain's National Union of Women's Suffrage Societies (1897) at over 50,000. And in 1924 NUSEC reported 163 affiliated societies, while the LWV had recruited about 65,000 members. Feminists, critics noted, were better at attracting middle-class women than their working-class sisters; yet as we saw in Chapter 2, working-class involvement increased as the women's movements matured, and it was honestly sought. We still know too little about the rank and file supporters of these movements, and of every other reform movement. But it does seem clear that in England they were numerous in London, where social problems abounded and lobby groups gathered to influence the national legislature, and in the parts of the country – notably the Midlands and the North – where women's employment had been transformed by industrialization and labour organizers were active. They were also significant among the networks linked by family ties, nonconformist and evangelical religion, radical politics, middle-class morality and frequently urban location, that sustained the national reforming tradition (Harrison 1980). In the United States, the movement's members were originally concentrated in the small towns and cities of the East and Midwest, but social feminism soon developed in all the major regions and suffragism had penetrated even the South by the end of the nineteenth century. In both countries, feminists were liable to be members of more than one group, and this overlapping membership helped to knit the elements of the cause together even as it spread the time of some activists rather thin.

Although there is always a danger that reform leaders will drift out of touch with their supporters, this does not appear to have been an especially serious problem for feminists. Leaders sometimes complained about the quietism of followers and of having to do too much themselves. Yet more retiring spirits were needed to provide an encouraging audience and regular subscriptions, while many workers behind the scenes played an invaluable part in managing the practical details of campaigns, as well as supplying hospitality and companionship for the leaders. An activist like the unmarried American suffragist, Susan B. Anthony, who spent long periods on the lecture circuit, could call upon a network of helpers, sometimes affluent, to make the travel, repetition and fatigue worthwhile (Harper 1983). The unquestioning loyalty ultimately demanded by the militant English suffragettes, Emmeline and Christabel Pankhurst, seems generally to have been neither expected nor given. Everyone recalls that one of their followers, Emily Davison, threw herself before the king's horse at the Derby in 1913 to publicize the cause. But though Davison was sustained by a cluster of militant comrades, her fatal gesture was an entirely personal initiative and a unique occurrence in the British and American feminist movements (Morley & Stanley 1988). For the vast majority of women who joined them, there were less dramatic rewards than martyrdom: principally companionship in a group larger than the family, and the stimulation of activities beyond home and convention.

As far as tactics are concerned, it was more important to be effective than to be original. Accordingly, feminists produced speeches, petitions, pamphlets, material for the press and specialist journals. They courted influential men, sought cross-party support, addressed meetings and mounted electoral campaigns. As they gained confidence, however, and trusted techniques went stale, activists became more inventive and adventurous. Since women were expected to be retiring, decorous and dependent, it is not surprising that a number of feminists welcomed the opportunity for fun, excitement and visibility. And so they took their meetings from the parlour to the public hall, and from the public hall to the streets. In the temperance, suffrage and labour groups in particular, attention was given to training women as organizers, speakers and recruiters, and since women were well established as writers and artists, it is understandable that they excelled in the literary and visual presentation of their message. On the whole, the English felt they made the most prudent organizers and investigators, and the Americans felt their educational and political system produced the best orators and agitators. It was therefore something of a surprise when a wing of the British suffrage campaign seized the attention of the world by its militant activities, which were eventually carried across the Atlantic.

The disagreement among historians about the wisdom of such activities has been nearly as great as the disagreement among the suffragists themselves. With roots in Anglo-American debates of the 1890s, militancy included tax resistance, mass demonstrations, publicity stunts and, late in the day, violence: usually against property but occasionally against the person (Bliss 1962; Rosen 1974; Holton 1980, 1994b; Harrison 1982; Evans 1984). It has provoked censure in the British context as requiring an impossible degree of escalation to sustain its shock effect, and for confirming enemies in their view that women were unfit to vote. Militancy was further undermined because the behaviour of the Pankhursts became unattractively auto-cratic while their followers, unlike those of feminist groups generally, could be highly undiplomatic in their indictment of men. American militants have been criticized because their attacks on the Wilson administration during the First World War made them look unpatri-otic, while their tactic of holding the party in power responsible for the failure to achieve women's suffrage was inappropriate in the American political system, where power was usually shared between the parties in Congress, and a president's ability to secure his party's programme was limited.

While militancy will be discussed further in Chapter 5, it is worth adding here that historians and contemporaries alike have played down the authorities' acts of violence against militants and high-lighted the involvement of privileged women in extreme tactics. Had militancy been favoured by working-class women, for whom it was normally an unacceptable risk, the response to it might have been different. In the eyes of many contemporary feminists, militancy was also at odds with the womanly style that they proudly employed, from preference and to distinguish their endeavours from those of male politicians. Women who enjoyed occasions graced with music, flowers and polite exchanges, and organizations free from unseemly wrangles over office, did not warm to the apparent abandonment of women's culture for that of men, whatever the reasons advanced for the change. Yet no amount of public politeness could guard women against the splits that disturb all reform movements. If the level of schisms in the last stages of British militant suffragism was not matched in any other branch of feminism, British social purists dis-agreed over how far the state should intervene to safeguard public morality, British suffragists differed over whether to pursue partial or adult suffrage, American temperance workers had divergent views about the wisdom of allying with political parties, and American feminists argued peculiarly passionately over the merits of protective industrial legislation.

Looking back at any reform movement, the historian will find omissions to ponder, emphases to question. The growing preoccu-pation with winning the vote has been widely regretted but equally widely exaggerated. Activists' neglect of sexual questions was once accepted but is now contested, and one reason for early assumptions was the lack of feminist organizations dedicated to campaigning in this area. When family planning groups were formed in the 1920s they cultivated independence, respectability, and the involvement of health professionals, being supported but not controlled by feminist and labour associations that were interested in a range of issues. The caution of all concerned demonstrates how controversial sexual matters still were. Before the 1920s they were frequently tackled incidentally by feminists, socialists, doctors and politicians, in discussions about divorce, the control of venereal disease and prostitution, the birthrate and maternal health.

The increasing institutionalization of reform and co-option of women into party politics during our period should not detract from the achievements of outstanding individual feminists, who owed little to substantial organizational backing. Activists continued to draw sustenance from close friendships and networks of personal contacts, such supports proving crucial to American women as late as the New Deal. And for those who despaired of progress in their own country, or rightly stressed the universality of many aspects of female oppression, there was from the 1880s the opportunity of joining an international woman's organization. These bodies were particularly attractive to American feminists, whose opportunities for imperial service were less than those of English women. The World's WCTU was established in 1884, the International Council of Women in 1888, the International Woman Suffrage Association in 1904, the Women's International League for Peace and Freedom in 1915, the Open Door International in 1929, and the World Woman's Party in 1938. If such associations did not always leave national prejudices at home, their existence is testimony to the activists' desire to make feminism something more than a narrowly focused movement, speaking to and for its dominant white Protestant elite (Foster 1989; Bosch & Kloosterman 1990; Tyrell 1991; Bacon 1993; Rupp 1994). However, reform movements almost never muster sufficient organizational power to offer a major challenge to the established institutions of the society they wish to transform. Feminism was no exception, finding politics and the professions, the family and the economy, stubbornly resistant to substantive change.

The leaders of the women's movements were none the less undaunted, impressive and invaluable. Social historians in the twentieth century have paid increasing attention to the lives of groups of women; but in the nineteenth century, when history was held to be made by the well-recorded few, it was necessary to demonstrate the existence of outstanding women. Although they were well aware that a "certain odium has ever rested on those who have risen above the conventional level" (*History of woman suffrage*, I, 1881), feminists were anxious both to place themselves in history and to take comfort from it in present struggles for advancement. They were determined to escape from the generalizations that lumped all women together and made leadership a masculine trait. Since the Scriptures were used to justify female subordination, it was important to refer to biblical heroines, and to a whole range of persecuted yet indomitable women of the past. Hence the names of St Scholastica, St Clara, St Catherine of Siena and St Bridget of Sweden were celebrated alongside those of male saints (Davis 1871), while Joan of Arc was held up as a model of courageous resistance (Tickner 1987). And until Victoria's death in 1901, the English activists were able to point out the irony of denying women political rights when the country was ruled by a queen. It is no accident that the publications on eminent women by Millicent Fawcett included a study of Queen Victoria, whom she believed could benefit the feminist cause, not least by demonstrating that public exertion and private domesticity were compatible (Rubinstein 1991).

Some of the individuals publicized by feminists were pioneers: women who had blazed a trail in a field not associated with their sex or one closed to it. They might help the feminist movement by their example and prestige rather than by active participation in feminist debates and organizations. Florence Nightingale, who transformed English nursing, and Clara Barton, who drew America into the International Red Cross and helped to broaden its mandate, would be obvious examples of such inspirational women in the nineteenth century (Pryor 1987; Baly 1988). Margaret Sanger and Marie Stopes, whose efforts led to the setting up of birth control clinics in the United States and England respectively, have a similar significance in the twentieth century (Kennedy 1970; Hall 1978). Yet historians have found plenty of fully involved feminist leaders as subjects for individual and group biographies (Lagemann 1979; Riegel 1980; Boyd 1982; Forster 1986; Harrison 1987; Alberti 1989; Caine 1992). And if Victorian women on each side of the Atlantic often wrote religious memoirs that abdicated self and elevated spiritual progress, or produced autobiographies that struggled to make themselves accessible to the majority of women who lived private lives, feminists themselves have left us with life stories that illuminate women's public roles. In their desire to justify the single state for women and to demonstrate the significance of the women's movement, they were frequently as willing as male autobiographers to emphasize their own achievements (Stanton 1898; Cobbe 1904; Fawcett 1924; Swanwick 1935; Pethick-Lawrence 1938; Bondfield 1949; Wells 1970; Pankhurst 1977; Addams 1981; Caine 1992; Flint 1993).

There was no single type of feminist leader in England or the United States, despite the inclination of opponents to caricature them as strident, mannish, unappealing, peculiarly dressed, and rootless because probably unmarried. Of course reformers of all kinds have ever been accused of oddness, mental and physical, and feminists were bound to encounter particular censure, given the strength of traditional opinion about feminine characteristics. But in fact the leaders of both the English and American women's movements were married as well as single, diplomatic as well as assertive, moderate as well as radical, interested in the comforts of home when they could be enjoyed, and usually concerned to present themselves acceptably.

The rational dress campaigns that arose periodically in feminism up to the First World War seldom involved its best known advocates, after they had learned early, in the United States, that bloomer costumes diverted attention from women's words to their appearance, where it had been customarily fixed. It thus proved necessary, as Mrs Stanton ruefully recalled, to sacrifice "freedom to repose" (quoted in Griffith 1984). There were a few activists whose presence could dismay those with a preference for wheedling femininity, among them the influential Anglo-Irish writer, Frances Power Cobbe; the uncompromising English and American crusaders for women's higher education, Emily Davies and M. Carey Thomas; and the suffragists Lydia Becker and Flora Drummond in England, and Susan Anthony and Anna Shaw in the United States. However, feminists were well aware that good looks helped their advocacy and made use of them where they could. Accordingly, Miss Davies was prepared to place attractive women at the front of meetings, to sweeten whatever unattractive propositions might be coming from the platform (Bennett 1990). Furthermore, any inspection of the leaders' portraits, especially before the achievement of dress reform in the interwar years of the twentieth century, reveals their interest in feminine, if respectable, clothing; their pleasure in striking jewellery, pretty collars and well-groomed hair.

This is not to say that feminist leaders could escape the stigma of peculiarity in their own time, and all of them had human foibles and weaknesses. Since women were expected to marry and perpetuate the race, it was not useful that there were more single activists by the early twentieth century, as women's opportunities for earning a living increased. Alarm was occasioned, too, by the fact that those who did marry tended to have small families or even no children. Mrs Stanton's seven offspring were unusual among feminists, and a challenge to independence that even her "noble, self-sacrificing" housekeeper of 30 years, Amelia Willard, could not minimize (Stanton 1898). The relations of married feminist women to their husbands, explored further in the next chapter, might also be atypical. Equally, single leaders were often made remarkable by the female friends who provided them with support.

These friends might be co-workers in the cause, financial backers, or allies in a conventional, "wifely" sense; but such partners' sexual relations, if any, have prompted more speculation among modern scholars than they did among contemporaries, since notwithstanding the writing of sexologists, lesbianism was not a widely discussed issue. Notable in this context are the relationships in America between Jane Addams and the affluent settlement house supporter Mary Rozet Smith; the Wellesley College academics Vida Scudder and Florence Converse; the political activist Molly Dewson and the reformist Polly Porter; and Pauline Newman and Frieda Miller of the Women's Bureau. In England, there were similar friendships between, among others, Frances Cobbe and one-time sculptor Mary Lloyd; Esther Roper and Eva Gore-Booth; the widowed American-born suffragist Elizabeth Robins and the doctor Octavia Wilberforce; and Eleanor Rathbone and fellow feminist Elizabeth Macadam (Faderman 1981; Ware 1987; Alberti 1989; Caine 1992; John 1995). An atypical transatlantic connection existed between Frances Willard and her English counterpart, Lady Henry Somerset, for loving partnerships are obviously difficult to sustain across national boundaries, and British and American temperance women soon resented the frequent absences of their leaders in another country.

English and American feminist leaders had other features in

common. In each country, there were some differences between activists according to generation, most notably in the interwar years of the twentieth century, with attitudes changing about the importance of the vote, the usefulness of protective legislation for women, and the centrality of sexual freedom to female emancipation. In each country, it was vital to produce national and local leaders, and they did emerge in social feminism and equal rights feminism alike. For working-class women, in particular, inexperience in reform, family commitments and lack of funds might render activism in their own community the only practical option. But the Americans' vast federal system made a network of leaders outside the capital essential, whatever their class, and they took a fierce pride in their independence: Western suffrage leaders resented visits by Eastern dignitaries bent on interference and in Frances Willard's judgement, the national WCTU had "not the slightest control over its state presidents" (Ida Husted Harper Papers).

While it is clear that practical women might be interested in ideas and ideologues might involve themselves in campaigning, each country nurtured high profile organization women like Becker and Anthony, Somerset and Willard, Fawcett and Catt. Each had their outstanding exponents of ideas, including Frances Power Cobbe and Elizabeth Stanton, Olive Schreiner and Charlotte Perkins Gilman. Each witnessed clashes between leaders of different types within single campaigns, most conspicuously in suffragism, where the methods of Becker, Fawcett, Anthony and Catt were anathema to the more uncompromising and unrestrained Pankhursts in England and to Lucy Burns and Alice Paul in the twentieth-century American movement. In both countries, spokeswomen noted for their unwavering idealism, emotionalism or contempt for convention experienced similarly difficult lives, though contrary to popular conception, such individuals are rare in reform endeavours rather than the norm. Emmeline Pankhurst and her daughter Christabel were fortunate to be sustained by their mutual admiration and loyalty. Less happy in their experiences were Sylvia Pankhurst; Charlotte Perkins Gilman; the intolerant English feminist thinker Teresa Billington Greig; and the labour activists and sex radicals, Annie Besant in England and Emma Goldman in the United States. The sexually adventurous Claflin sisters found serenity only when they left America and secured respectable English husbands and interests. Finally, the

61

significant English and American feminists were well acquainted from the beginning of their crusade, communication being facilitated by correspondence, visits, published progress reports and the international women's associations. Mrs Fawcett was unusual in her refusal to cross the Atlantic, despite invitations from American suffragists and her enthusiasm for travel (Rubinstein 1991). As a staunch patriot, she may have preferred to keep her eyes firmly fixed on the national scene, and her obduracy is a useful reminder that feminists in the two countries were determined to preserve their independence and special characteristics, however close their ties.

In seeking a new deal for women, feminists in England and the United States did not see the need for novelty in all matters. Just as their tactics were generally conventional, so their leaders perforce had much in common with male leaders, both needing to cultivate publicity, good connections, loyal supporters, persuasive ideas, and the courage of their convictions. None the less, their frequent avoidance of involvement in party politics until after the vote was won, and of the personality cult in favour of an emphasis upon issues and womanly conduct, constituted a considered attempt to realize women's claims to moral superiority and distinctiveness from men. Even where bitter disagreements and schisms erupted, they did not result in public, one-to-one slanging matches between the key protagonists. Despite the embarrassment caused by the unfeminine militancy of the Pankhursts, for instance, Mrs Fawcett long defended their approach to non-suffragists and confided to one of her allies in 1909, "I don't feel it is the right thing and yet the spectacle of so much self-sacrifice moves people to activity who would otherwise sit still and do nothing" (Fawcett Library Autograph Letter Collection).

The differences between English and American feminist leaders are not numerous, but they are significant. They are related to the particular preoccupations of the two movements, outlined in this chapter, and to the different class and racial challenges their activists encountered, examined in Chapter 2. Perhaps because their class position convinced them that they could take charge of anything that interested them, more upper-class women became leaders of the women's movement in Britain than in the United States (albeit they were a small minority in either country). Conspicuous among them were the art historian and labour activist, Lady Emilia Dilke; Frances Power Cobbe, whose upbringing as an unmarried daughter in an important Anglo-Irish family contributed at once to her confidence and her indignation about the treatment of women; the busy Liberal Unionist suffragist Lady Frances Balfour, who made good use of her political connections as the sister-in-law of A. J. Balfour, the eventual Conservative premier; and Lady Nancy Astor, the first woman to sit in parliament and a feminist interested in a wide range of issues, though never driven only by her feminism (Banks 1986; Harrison 1987; Levine 1990; Caine 1992). Yet more significant in Britain, and not paralleled in the United States, was the group of leaders who emerged with an interest in launching cross-class associations to benefit women, and who found that they and their outstanding labour allies were forced apart after the First World War. This unfortunate development was the result of a determined effort by the male dominated Labour Party to secure for class causes the undivided allegiance of its female supporters, and of middle-class feminists' disgust at the party's failure to push reforms on behalf of women (Graves 1994). That the British feminist movement produced no settlement house workers, temperance advocates and club women who were as well known as the American leaders in those fields, simply reflects their greater importance for American feminists. And of course the difficulties of women of colour in the American movement denied them the luxury of a large range of leadership types. Of necessity, non-white feminist leaders were practical as well as idealistic.

Historians of women have been concerned to point up female differences in recent years. But it is worth concluding this chapter by emphasizing what, apart from specific campaigns and organizational ties, drew diverse women together. Among the feminist movement's best known intellectuals, Elizabeth Stanton came from a prosperous New York family, learned about injustice from her father's legal profession, received a good education and was exposed early to the influence of reformers. Married at 24 to one of them and largely held to domestic duties until she was in her fifties, Mrs Stanton then added to her reputation as a brilliant but intermittent speaker and writer on women's issues by taking to the lecture circuit for ten years. Though ultimately cushioned by a legacy from her father, she stretched herself to the utmost without ever losing her pleasure in company, novels, food, games and naps. On the face of it, she had little in common with Frances Cobbe, who came to feminism via philanthropy, private reflection and foreign travel, and was a political conservative. Both women may be contrasted against the writer Olive Schreiner, brought up by strict missionary parents, marrying late and unsuccessfully, losing her only child, and frequently isolated in South Africa from the main centres of feminist debate (First & Scott 1980). And all three differed in temper and lifestyle from Charlotte Perkins Gilman who, while blessed with distinguished New England ancestors, was the product of a broken home, reared by an unsympathetic mother, frequently on the move, and quickly acquainted with the need to earn a living. This she did at the expense of her first marriage and, to some extent her daughter, whose care she yielded to her divorced husband and his second wife.

What these women did share was, however, considerable. All encountered domestic difficulties as they grew to maturity: the family circle that was meant to provide them with everything was found wanting and restrictive. They were all able to engage imaginatively with women far less fortunate than themselves and therefore to speak on their behalf. All were bold enough to confront sexual questions and the double standard, to emphasize women's economic subordination, and to relate feminism to the important intellectual currents of their time. All recognized that female emancipation required action on many fronts, and believed that women, despite their faults, were equal to the challenge.

CHAPTER FOUR

Anti-feminists and feminist men

The women's movements, like all major social movements, provoked fierce criticism that was at once diffused throughout society and given focus by specific, self-interested groups. As a result, feminists spent considerable time on repudiating – and so publicizing – the arguments of opponents, when they would have preferred to concentrate on the positive part of their message. Although the independent organization of anti-feminism was less impressive than that of the feminists, its adherents had the great advantage of defending that which seemed customary and therefore right, and were frequently blessed with affluence and social prominence. Under these circumstances, one would expect them to have had some effective arguments and to have secured some victories. But while they certainly did, the feminists at least held their own: neither side could claim overall victory.

It should be stressed at the outset that feminists and anti-feminists (or Antis, as they were called) had a number of beliefs in common. Both argued that women had a special role to play in the home, as wives, mothers and society's guardians of morality. Both accordingly celebrated women's domestic virtues. Both accepted that women were men's opposites in certain respects. However, there the two groups parted company. For whereas anti-feminists believed that women, with their smaller bodies and brains, were innately less strong, intelligent, rational and reliable than men, and uniquely dominated by their physical characteristics, feminists maintained that unfavourable environmental factors accounted for most differences between the sexes, and that women's physical weaknesses could be tackled or were grossly exaggerated. Whereas anti-feminists generalized about women's existing deficiencies in order to perpetuate them, feminists acknowledged some weaknesses in order to make their case for change (Harrison 1978).

Building on their view of what women were – a view that denied significant variety among them – Antis rejected the forces of modernity and stressed the importance of social stability and established authority. The changes urged by feminists would, they asserted, elude women or make them ill and unhappy. Either way, emancipated women would compete for men's jobs, alienate their male protectors, flout the biblical injunctions to women to be silent in public and serve their husbands, and deprive their communities of the benefits that had traditionally resulted from female piety, modesty and selflessness. What is more, it was alleged that the campaign for women's emancipation was linked to and would encourage other dangerous movements. In advancing such views, it is clear that anti-feminists disliked not only feminist goals but also the sort of women they associated with them: what the English author Eliza Lynn Linton dismissed as a "shrieking sisterhood", disagreeably unrestrained and indifferent to masculine claims and chivalry (Linton 1870). Yet if there was a strain of misogyny in anti-feminism, there was equally a desire to worship women, provided they would conform to type. Worshippers ranged from the followers of the positivist philosopher, Auguste Comte, who emphasized women's maternal, moral and religious roles at the expense of everything else, to the blunt anti-suffragist who exclaimed "My mother was a woman, my wife is a woman, I love them, bless them and I'd save them from the vote" (H. B. Laidlaw Papers).

Those feminists who put a premium on entering the public sphere were regarded with particular disfavour, and it is easy to see why. If men had some part to play in the domestic sphere, they were glad to leave it mainly to women. Yet if women were allowed to compete with men in the public sphere, Antis held that the one clear area of male dominance would have been surrendered, contrary to the Darwinist elevation of specialization. In an era of "differentiation and division of labour", they saw themselves as "the scientific and modern party" (Mrs Humphrey Ward, quoted in Sutherland 1990). Hence the anti-feminists felt justified in opposing female politicization. It was believed that women in the public realm, having too much to say and do, would shun marriage, resent child rearing, raise juvenile delinquents, and turn once tranquil families into worldly battlegrounds. They would, in addition, vote on the promptings of emotion rather than information, opt for persons over policies, quickly seek elevation to public office, and invade men's comfortable clubs. For British Antis there was the further anxiety that women voters would convince foreigners and colonial subjects that a once virile nation intended to convert "the whole world into an epicene institution" (Wright 1913).

At the beginning of our period, when voting was not done by private ballot, and rowdiness and corruption still accompanied elections, some Antis understandably feared that bringing women into politics would "brush the bloom off the flowers" (Bryce, II, 1889). While force might be a less important factor in securing political and social stability than it once was, it remained significant, especially to the British, because of "the immense increase of . . . [their] imperial responsibilities" (Mrs Humphrey Ward, quoted in Sutherland 1990). Accordingly, women were discomforted by the charge that they would not be able to back up their votes, or any laws they helped to secure, by force, should the need arise. It was not enough to respond that only a minority of men deployed force on behalf of the state; the point was that the minority was male. Yet in their apprehension at the prospect of women voting at the national political level, anti-feminists (like feminists) often claimed what they could not prove and contradicted themselves along the way (Harrison 1978; Pugh 1980; Kraditor 1981). It was asserted that the ballot was not worth much: that women would not vote and that their enfranchisement would change nothing. Conversely, voting was presented as a special "privilege of government" that only a few were given and fit to exercise (*History of woman suffrage*, VI, 1922). But it was added, the disgruntled and disreputable would be sure to vote if they could. Alternative nightmare scenarios were that women would weakly cast their ballots in response to masculine pressure, or would boldly cast them against such honest pleasures as drinking, thereby damaging the economy. Enfranchised women were envisaged as too conservative and too radical; as an unpredictable mass of individualistic voters and an all too predictable voting bloc. What could plainly be demonstrated, however, was that women as well as men were dismayed by feminism, and were prepared to organize against the enfranchisement of their sex, something that men did not do.

There were several reasons for female unease about the vote. The feminists at Seneca Falls in 1848, recognizing the radicalism of demanding the franchise, feared that they might make themselves ridiculous by including it among their aims. Social feminists seeking men's backing for their reforms and encouraged by legislators' growing willingness to respond, might initially avoid suffragism as an unrealistic campaign or an objective irrelevant to their own. Some might in time revise this view; cases in point being Josephine Butler, Emily Davies, Frances Willard, Lady Somerset, Beatrice Webb, and the pioneering doctor Elizabeth Blackwell. None the less, many reformist women remained uncomfortable with suffragists' faith in the transforming power of the vote and politics generally, and argued, like the American writer Ida Tarbell, that men and women were "widely apart in functions and in possibilities"; that the sexes could not "be made equal by exterior devices like trousers, ballots, [and] the study of Greek". Proud of women's traditional role, they shared Tarbell's belief that "necessity is what forces new tools into human hands – not argument and agitation" (Ida Tarbell Papers). Other women who joined the anti-suffrage associations seem to have been temperamentally opposed to militant campaigns, besides being satisfied with the influence that stemmed from their privileged position and fearful of feminism's threat to prevailing family arrangements. Women who belonged to political parties, as a growing minority did by the early twentieth century, might also put party priorities and attitudes to female enfranchisement before suffragist claims. Thus, for example, women socialists in England opposed as undemocratic suffragists' demand for the vote on the same terms as men, demanding adult suffrage instead; while women Democrats in the United States endorsed the party's determination not to reopen the question of black enfranchisement by considering female suffrage, support for which was seen as a Republican trait.

Since votes for women were resisted with extraordinary vehemence, it was understandable that organizations came into being to spread the anti-suffragists' arguments and keep politicians in line. They emerged first in America at the state level, operating from the time of the earliest efforts to admit women to the presidential franchise in the 1860s, normally disbanding once a suffragist campaign had been defeated and reviving only if suffragism revived in the area concerned. Apart from producing petitions, testifying at hearings, cultivating legislators and publishing literature of various kinds, these Antis investigated conditions in states where women had eventually won the vote, seeking to show that their enfranchisement was neither significant nor beneficial. Their endeavours spread to all the main regions of the United States, and from 1911 were strengthened by a National Association Opposed to Woman Suffrage. British opposition mustered inside and outside parliament as private members' bills were presented proposing women's suffrage; but given the difficulty of enacting such bills, the Antis did not feel the need for a national body until 1908, when the Women's National Anti-Suffrage League was founded. A Men's League for Opposing Women's Suffrage followed in 1909, and the two leagues amalgamated a year later, being named from 1911 the National League for Opposing Women's Suffrage. If the management of the Antis' affairs in parliament was not notably efficient, the achievements in the Women's League of Mrs Humphrey Ward, a social reformer and novelist, made a nonsense of the more disparaging anti-feminist charges against women (Rover 1967; Harrison 1978; Sutherland 1990; Camhi 1994; Jablonsky 1994).

Powerful groups as well as conservative individuals swelled the ranks of the Antis at different times. Clergymen were quickly offended by women's challenge to the authority of religious dogma and men's monopoly of the pulpit. In England they also disliked the female attempt to gain entry to Oxford and Cambridge, whose government they still dominated in the nineteenth century. Yet whereas Catholic opposition to female emancipation continued throughout our period, not least because of the growing feminist boldness on birth control and divorce, Protestant clerics tended to come to terms with activists whose reformist objectives often coincided with their own by the late nineteenth century. Educators in both countries at first condemned women's pursuit of equality with men as being unnecessary, unsuitable and unrealistic, given women's innate characteristics and domestic destiny. Male reformers frequently opposed women's entry into their domain, unless they were willing to confine themselves to womanly tasks, and feared that feminism could make matters worse for vulnerable women who needed man's protection in all aspects of their lives. Medical men before the twentieth century commonly criticized women activists who challenged their expert judgements about female brains and bodies, were associated with irregular opinions about birth control, abortion and health care, and inappropriately sought entry to the medical profession just as it was trying to improve its standards. But between the two world wars, doctors and feminists finally allied to make birth control respectable and more widely available, and the state of medical knowledge generally permitted a more harmonious relationship between the two groups.

If the passage of time could undermine the arguments and hostility of anti-feminists, they were never entirely routed. Hence during the 1920s, a decade of political reaction in Britain and America alike, old ideas about women's proper place flourished, despite their greater sexual freedom and enfranchisement; while during the 1930s, an era of mass unemployment, ancient prejudices against women working outside the home resurfaced, despite the high profile of American women in New Deal politics and agencies. The Antis held up the passage of female enfranchisement, obliged activists to proceed cautiously in the areas of educational and sexual reform, and contributed to the unattractive image of feminism that has endured to the present. Their conservatism did not, however, take identical forms on each side of the Atlantic. Although Irish Nationalist aversion to women's suffrage was an obstacle in parliament for several years, there was no British equivalent of the American South's long opposition to it, in and outside Congress, as an alien and modern demand that threatened state rights. There was no equivalent, in Britain, of the organized interests and "machine" politicians that rallied against women's suffrage; no equivalent of the opposition to it by immigrant groups, who were concerned with protecting rather than emancipating their women in an often alarming New World. American Antis were particularly hostile to the militancy of British suffragettes, which they saw as unnecessary in their more democratic country; while British Antis showed greater concern about the impact on women of improved education, not sharing the founding commitment of the United States to an educated citizenry and female instruction that transcended the decorative.

Finally, American anti-feminists usually rejected their British counterparts' distinction between unacceptable feminine participation in the masculine issues of national politics, and a fitting female involvement in the welfare issues that were so important at the local political level. Whereas in Britain parliament was supreme, and local government was frequently concerned merely with enacting its measures, in the United States the different tiers of government were sovereign in their own areas, so that women enjoying local political rights – as many did in the later nineteenth century – on the face of it were politicized in a more significant role. Alternatively American Antis may have recognized that suffragists in their country were even less likely to be contented with limited voting rights than English activists were. After all, white working men had been enfranchised since the 1850s, and white women had not flatteringly been drawn into local political work by major parties as they had in England. Mrs Catt summed up the hostile attitude of American suffragists when she complained that women anti-suffragists had acquired the "power of education, of property, of organization, of free speech, of partial political rights" through the efforts of others, yet said to suffragists "with supreme self-satisfaction . . . 'Thus far shalt thou come and no farther.' It takes no logic to perceive the inconsistency of such a position" (*History of woman suffrage*, VI, 1922).

If feminists found it hard to engage with such opponents, they found it far from easy to work out their relations with the men who influenced their lives and with those who actually favoured their cause. On the one hand, activists generally recognized the need to interest and convert men, to work with them for reform objectives, and to pay special attention to influential male legislators. It was equally obvious that unless they could manage their own campaigns, Antis would be confirmed in their view of women's limited capabilities. On the other hand, women varied in their personal preferences for male or female company, and in the degree to which they embraced claims about woman's moral superiority. Moreover, some feminists and male writers acknowledged that the secularized Victorian vision of masculinity, with its emphasis on strength, physical endurance, assertiveness and achievement, asked too much of men and generalized unhelpfully about them (Stearns 1979; Christ 1980; Leach 1981; Mangan & Walvin 1987). Modern observers have been still more concerned to show that masculinity, like femininity, was a creation of society and not a natural, unchanging entity (Lake 1986; Brod 1987; Kimmel 1987; Hyam 1990; Morgan 1992).

Whereas Antis were fearful that feminism would foster androgyny, feminist writers at the end of the century set out to create a "new man" to match the "new woman". Men, of course, could more easily reject their allotted social roles than women: male eccentrics were never so censured as their female counterparts, ascetic or high living bachelors were never so despised as careful or colourful spinsters. But the "new man" was to be defined neither by singlehood nor an interest in free love. Rather, he was recognizable by his willingness to accept women on their own terms (Showalter 1992). These terms were not set impossibly high. When questioning prevailing definitions of masculinity, feminists did not fashion an entirely novel concept of womanhood or demand role reversal from their male allies. Given the success with which middle-class notions of masculinity had been disseminated in Britain and America by the end of the nineteenth century through schools, universities, clubs, sport and the armed services, their caution was understandable (Mangan & Walvin 1987).

The men who influenced female activism did so by both positive and negative example, and white feminists, whose fathers' authority was supreme even in the domestic sphere, often recorded them as their main parental influence. Among the working-class suffragists who emerged in the North of England, Cissey Foley's radicalism owed something to her indignant perception of her father's failings as a husband and breadwinner, while Elizabeth Dean resented her father's sexual demands on her mother as contributing to her early death. Florence Nightingale adored her father but chafed at his opposition to her desire for independence until she was in her thirties. Emily Davies and Frances Cobbe had unsympathetic fathers, and only when they died was it possible wholeheartedly to embrace social activism. Elizabeth Stanton was mortified by her father's response to her childhood efforts to impress him as "learned and courageous": "Ah, you should have been a boy!" (Stanton 1898). On her journey towards feminism, Stanton's fellow countrywoman and eventual ideological opponent, Lucy Stone, vowed not to marry after witnessing the power wielded by her domineering father; and Emma Goldman grew up observing conflict between her parents, emigrating to America partly to escape her father's unappealing plans for her future. Women of colour, whose mothers were likely to have had to work for money and whose fathers suffered racial and economic discrimination, were far less liable than their white sisters to owe their start to well connected fathers. None the less, Beatrice Webb, Josephine Butler, Millicent Fawcett, the English suffragist Emmeline Pethick Lawrence, Susan Anthony, Jane Addams, the American feminist writer Caroline Dall, and the pioneer American doctors Harriot Hunt and Mary Putman Jacobi, are just a few of the feminists who were fortunate in the education, support or example that their fathers could give them. By contrast, conventional mothers could be a major problem for aspiring daughters (Hersh 1978; Liddington & Norris 1978; Riegel 1980; Smith-Rosenberg 1985; Banks 1986; Forster 1986; Caine 1992).

Feminists might also be sustained by beloved brothers or made envious of their better education and prospects. But their husbands were yet more important to leading activists. Besides reinforcing feminists' claims to respectable femininity, they assisted their wives by providing useful contacts, financial assistance, time-consuming moral support and, we must assume, backing for family limitation. Since everything has its price, it should be noted that the price for marriages in which the sexual and social interests of both parties was considered could include frequent separations, public ridicule and private tensions. Women felt guilty about being away from home, by no means all children of such unions became reformers themselves, and the separated partners either pined for each other or grew apart.

Activists like Josephine Butler in England, and Harriet Laidlaw, Ethel Dreier, Mary Terrell, Catharine McCulloch and Lillie Devereux Blake in America, discovered that absence did make the heart grow fonder, and they were consequently driven to lecture on a variety of feminist issues from necessity rather than inclination. Their husbands' pride in them helped to keep such women on the road. Hence on receiving a remittance from his wife when she was away, Frank McCulloch asked, "Can't I brag of my wife now, and tell how she is supporting me. I'll show those folks that don't like suffragists that they don't know what they are talking about" (C. G. W. McCulloch Papers); and Robert Terrell exhorted his wife not to be downcast "by the jealousies and envy of those who don't like you because you are doing something in the world" (Mary Church Terrell Papers). Other feminists, including Elizabeth Stanton, Charlotte Gilman, Carrie Catt and Millicent Fawcett, found that an independent feminist career came only with estrangement from their husbands or with widowhood. And women who married late, having first established their feminist credentials, could find, like Ida Wells, that their supporters felt they had "deserted the cause" (Wells 1970).

Perhaps the best known feminist union was that between John Stuart Mill and Harriet Taylor, formalized after the death of Harriet's first husband but following a long marriage of true minds. Commentators in and beyond Mill's own day have found it difficult to accept as fair his tribute to his wife's "clear, powerful, original, and comprehensive intellect", that made her "the guide and support, the instructor in wisdom, and the example in goodness . . . of those who had the happiness to belong to her". Almroth Wright accordingly devoted several pages of his blast against women's suffrage to a condemnation of Mill, denouncing both his personal identification with women's lot and his tendency to set up an abstract version of femininity that he could then demolish. While some of Mill's *Subjection of women* is indeed too generalized and his personal experiences certainly do underpin the work, Wright's complaint fails to do justice either to Mill's intellectual toughness, or to the fruitfulness of his intellectual collaboration with a woman more radical than he was on the issue of female emancipation (Wright 1913; Mill & Mill 1970; Tulloch 1984).

The largest number of feminism's male supporters seem to have been located in the hard fought suffrage movement, though the sexes also worked together for educational advances, social purity and peace, for reform of the marriage laws and, eventually, to improve women's economic prospects and social welfare. English women, never having developed the American tradition of powerful female conventions to demand reform, were on the whole more ready to accept this co-operation positively. As the *English Woman's Journal* expressed it in 1858, "There is a strength in unity, which, as far as the male and female element is concerned, the world has yet to test" (vol. I, no. 4). American feminists had, however, divided over the degree of influence to accord to men as early as 1848, and differed substantially on the question by the time they established their first suffrage societies in the 1860s. In consequence, followers of Lucy Stone in the American Woman Suffrage Association courted Republican and abolitionist backing, and were keen to recruit "prominent and able men" (DuBois 1978); whereas Elizabeth Stanton's allies in the American Woman Suffrage Association favoured an organization dominated by women, since by "standing alone we learned our power" (*History of woman suffrage*, II, 1881).

When the suffrage campaign had made some progress, women recognized the need to broaden the base of their support, successfully reaching out to particular occupational groups, working-class women, and men from all backgrounds. Tribute was paid in America to the work of men's leagues for women suffrage, and men of property and standing were especially targeted because of the money and prestige they could bring to the movement, and because they usually had the time and confidence to stage events and debate the case with well placed opponents. The *History of woman suffrage* conceded that "Behind many a woman who worked there was a man aiding and sustaining her with money and personal sacrifice. 'Suffrage husbands' became a title of distinction" (VI, 1922). A similar situation prevailed in England, and is epitomized in Frederick Pethick Lawrence's determination that women should "not be left to fight this battle alone" (quoted in Harrison 1987). A man of wealth, opposed equally to oppression on the grounds of sex, class or colour, he encouraged his wife's independent activities and helped the suffragettes with money, editorial skills, advice, a willingness to go to gaol for his beliefs, and the tact not to make public his bitter feelings about being expelled, together with his wife, from the Pankhurst-dominated Women's Social and Political Union. Furthermore, Pethick Lawrence continued to speak out on women's issues during his career as a Labour MP between the two world wars (Brittain 1963; Hale 1974; Harrison 1987; Morgan 1992).

If the existence of such men proved it was possible to be a male feminist, they did not lead the women's movement or form more than a small minority of its supporters. Their presence was particularly helpful in the early days of the movement, when allies were hardest to find. They seemed less vital once women's roles broadened and they had acquired considerable expertise as activists, though sympathetic men were always needed in the political realm, where women never had the power of numbers. In both countries, male allies tended to be drawn from the liberal-left end of the political spectrum, but in Britain, after the vote had been won, the determination of working men to anchor working women firmly within the socialist rather than the feminist movement was damaging to feminism. Men who had been drawn into suffragism via their own separate organizations were under no pressure to continue working with women after female enfranchisement, and the motives that led men into feminism could determine the extent of their usefulness to their women allies. Love or admiration for specific women, chivalry towards the many (which was not confined to Antis), an outraged sense of justice, or reform interests shared with women, might not be enough to make men more than partially committed to the cause (Strauss 1982; Banks 1986; Harrison 1987; Morgan 1992).

The men in the feminist movement did not encounter as much hostility as the women. They might have asserted themselves in an outlandish fashion, but assertion for political ends was acceptable male behaviour (Morgan 1992). Their involvement in feminism nevertheless required real courage, as other men reacted to dismaying social changes and personal challenges by stressing what made them different from women. Feminists acknowledged that they must do the main work of emancipation, and cultivated female support networks to make the work bearable. Yet they were cheered along the way by the knowledge that all men need not be their enemies.

CHAPTER FIVE

Activism, c.1870–1918

Education

If the English and American women's movements had a wide array of goals, they made their first gains in areas where they did not immediately threaten men's power and comfort, and where they could enlist the support of other reformers and the state. Education – at least up to college level – was one of those areas. In the United States, it was endorsed by parents, politicians, moralists, prosperous citizens, labour leaders and educators anxious to civilize the West, assimilate immigrants, ensure an intelligent electorate, provide a focus for local communities, and guarantee the nation's economic progress. In England, male curriculum reformers, aspiring women teachers, politicians, employers and parents variously saw the point of adapting education to take account of industrialization, professional and bureaucratic changes, the extension of the suffrage, a female "surplus" in the population, and delayed marriage in the middle class.

It was thus in a social climate favourable to change that women on each side of the Atlantic reworked the utilitarian arguments for education circulating in their day, and based on the assumption that men and women had different characteristics and destinies. Accordingly, activists maintained that improving women's instruction would safeguard their morals, make them more effective mothers and teachers, and enhance their appeal as wives in the companionate marriages lauded by the middle class. Less ingratiatingly, feminists also hoped that educated women would be more questioning, ambitious and impressive; and hence that they would lose what the Oxford educated novelist, Winifred Holtby, termed their "nasty little inferiority complexes" (quoted in Leonardi 1989).

American and English activists had their own emphases and shaping influences within this broad debate. Feminists in England were particularly prone to stress the economic importance of enhanced female education, including vocational training. They were strongly affected by their class background, devoting most of their time to the needs of middle-class girls and women. And they were obliged to mount a long campaign for admission to England's two ancient universities: Oxford did not open its degrees and government to women until 1920, while Cambridge held out until 1948. Since these institutions had for centuries and without challenge recruited the sons of the privileged to groom them for their role as the nation's next social and political elite, such opposition was to be expected. The leading American universities never quite acquired comparable power.

American feminists, by contrast, could draw on a national ethos that exalted education and equality of opportunity. Consequently seminaries (or secondary schools) for girls had been founded early in the young republic. The size of America and the need to expand educational facilities quickly led to the creation of co-educational establishments at every level, thereby increasing female opportunities to break down male prejudices at first hand. Moreover, the loss of men during the Civil War (1861–5), and the rebuilding of the devastated South during the ensuing period of Reconstruction (1865–77), created exceptional opportunities for American women teachers. On the other hand, women's education proceeded slowly in the southern states, which were poorer, less populous and more conservative than their northern neighbours. In addition, for people of colour throughout America there was a constant struggle to secure their fair share of educational appropriations, to raise private funding, and to resist being steered towards vocational education regardless of inclination.

Because they worked with other groups for educational reform, the achievements of feminists are hard to isolate. But it seems clear that on this, as on so many topics, they played a vital part in challenging accepted claims and practices. They were influential in publicizing women's successes, with a view to proving their educability.

Similarly, they gathered and circulated data to refute medical and Darwinist arguments about women's permanent mental inferiority, and to repudiate allegations that severe mental exertion endangered girls' future maternal roles. Feminists were frequently forged through education, finding personal satisfaction, independence and female friendships from their experiences. They sought better provision for others, and were not deterred by their disagreements, notably over the desirability of separate educational facilities and curricula for the sexes. Whereas some activists believed that female schools and colleges ensured propriety, freedom from male hostility and exposure to women role models, and questioned the timeless relevance of instruction in the liberal arts, others feared that unless women succeeded in traditional subjects they would not be seen as men's equals, and that separate facilities might be few in number, isolating and underfunded. Despite such differences, feminists were united in seeing women's admission to college instruction as imperative if they were ever to challenge the masculine monopoly of the best paid, professional jobs.

American feminists campaigned for the admission of women to established universities (such as Michigan), and influenced the radicalization of the separate colleges for women (such as Vassar, 1865; Wellesley and Smith, 1875; and Bryn Mawr, 1884). They took part in the creation of co-ordinate female colleges attached to elite institutions that would not admit women (such as Radcliffe, linked to Harvard from 1879), and sought the acceptance of women as equal participants in new foundations (such as Boston University, 1873). By 1890, women constituted approximately 36 per cent of the American undergraduate population. English activists had more to do, since educational provision for women lagged behind that of the United States at every level in 1870. Hence they strove, successfully, to prove that girls could pass the examinations set by universities to test school leavers. When the quality of boys' secondary instruction was debated during the 1860s, feminists helped to persuade the resulting Taunton Commission (1864–8) to examine the condition of girls' schools. They worked with others for the establishment of new female secondary schools, and of colleges for women at Cambridge (Girton, 1869; Newnham, 1871) and Oxford (Somerville and Lady Margaret Hall, 1879; St Hugh's, 1886; St Hilda's, 1893). Their efforts may have influenced the expanding English provincial universities to admit women. As members of the school boards set up in 1870 to administer the new state supported primary schools, feminists had the opportunity to learn additional political skills and make much needed contacts with working-class communities. And in the United States and England alike, they supported physical education for girls and women as a way of contesting notions about female frailty.

There were, of course, disappointments and deficiencies. In 1894, the English journal *Punch* warned the "new woman" to

> ... be not stupid,
> Fight not with Hymen and war not with Cupid.

Activists found it impossible to destroy ancient convictions that women's education should fit them for domesticity; indeed, it was often thought imprudent to try. Such beliefs were strengthened in both countries by Darwinism and eugenicism. They were given a further boost in England by particularly strong class prejudices, and a desire to see women playing their part in sustaining the imperial race and the British Empire. Nor could feminists dispel the conviction in dominant male universities that female students were a threat to academic standards and agreeable masculine ways. Female secondary school and college graduates (never numerous in England) were also likely to find a use for their qualifications only in occupations thought to be suitable for women, namely teaching, nursing, librarianship, clerical and social work. In these sex typed and segregated jobs, they were poorly placed to build on the radicalizing features of their education but powerful enough to come into conflict with unpaid women philanthropists.

The educational struggle itself consumed much female energy for most of our period. If women coveted a career in academic life, they faced a shortage of funds, postgraduate and job opportunities. Moreover, outside schools for girls, they saw the top posts go to men. Far from uniting women across class and race lines, educational campaigns confirmed the limits of sisterhood: their chief beneficiaries were white and middle class. The fact that education was seen as the key to a variety of advances for women made activists avoid alarming alliances with other feminists and shun unwomanly tactics. The female students who gained from improved facilities were likewise constrained by the need to behave decorously, frequently putting prudence before that freedom to question and dare that is an essential part of a good education. When many educated women failed to marry, or married late and had few children, the fears of conservatives of both sexes were confirmed (Talbot & Rosenberry 1931; Rogers 1938; Woody 1966; Holcombe 1973; McWilliams-Tullberg 1975, 1980; Delamont & Atkinson 1978; Graham 1978; Bryant 1979; Ellsworth 1979; Pederson 1979; Burstyn 1980; Fletcher 1980; Dyhouse 1981; Rosenberg 1982; Horowitz 1984; Solomon 1985; Vicinus 1985; Rubinstein 1986; Hollis 1987; McCrone 1988; Bennett 1990; Tyack & Hansot 1990; Avery 1991; Purvis 1991).

The economy

In the economic and political arenas, women lacked the allies they found in the educational sphere. Feminists in both countries made a courageous case for women's right to work, for the good of themselves and society. They publicized first the lack of jobs available to women, regardless of class, and then the positions that were opening up by the later nineteenth century. They also effectively linked women's narrow range of economic options to inadequate education and training, and graphically depicted the loveless marriages and prostitution that might ensnare women without means to support themselves. But in a country ruled by market forces, American activists did not find organizational means to produce more job openings for members of the middle class; and although the British were driven by their awareness of the "surplus" woman problem to establish a Society for Promoting the Employment of Women, modest resources limited its usefulness. Furthermore, if feminists on each side of the Atlantic campaigned for entry to the established men's professions, until the interwar years of the twentieth century they had little impact on occupations whose conditions of employment were unhelpful to women and whose members opposed their admission. Undeterred, activists made the medical profession their major focus.

It was accurately argued that women had always been associated with health care, and that as doctors they might appeal to other women because of their special knowledge of female bodies and sensibilities. Institutions were prevailed upon to open their doors to women medical students – from the 1840s in the United States and the 1870s in England. However, they naturally admitted non-feminists as well as feminists, as did the women's medical schools set up by women in both countries. After the early pioneering days, female students accepted for a medical course were likely to find that the pressures on them were primarily professional. The years of instruction, long hours and regular moves required of fledgling doctors none the less militated against women physicians who aspired to family life, and worked against the feminist case that medicine was an appropriate field for women. Even the happily married and reformist American doctor Mary Putnam Jacobi acknowledged that "a physician owed entire devotion to the profession" (Mary Putnam Jacobi Papers). While female doctors sometimes provided valuable ammunition against male practitioners who exaggerated female weaknesses, they could not be relied upon to do so. Margaret Cleaves, MD, of Des Moines, confessed in 1886 that she had entered medicine to please her father, only to find herself the victim of a "sprained brain". She predicted that whereas a few women might succeed in assuming men's roles, "shattered nerves" would be the experience of the majority (quoted in Haller & Haller 1974). What is more, female doctors never enjoyed the power of numbers, constituting 6 per cent of the medical profession in America in 1910, and 1.98 per cent of the total in England and Wales in 1911 (Bell 1953; Manton 1965; Wilson 1970; Shryock 1972; Holcombe 1973; L'Esperance 1977; Walsh 1977; Harrison 1981; Smith-Rosenberg 1985; Solomon 1985).

The involvement of middle-class women in other parts of the economy owed as much to expanding demand for workers deemed to be cheap and manageable as it did to pressures from female reformers. Dislike of middle-class women taking paid jobs was eroded but not destroyed by the knowledge that many were obliged to do so; and when they were active outside the home, such women were uncomfortably aware that their activism was facilitated by the labours of female servants. Accordingly, by the late nineteenth century socialist feminists in England and the United States had turned their attention to the possibility of replacing the old, divisive housekeeping arrangements by paid, professionalized or co-operative housework. Apartments and grouped houses with communal kitchens, dining rooms, laundries and crèches would, it was urged, create worthwhile jobs for women of domestic bent and emancipate those who were not. They might, in addition, solve the "servant problem" – that is the scarcity of servants, which was particularly marked in the libertarian United States. Unfortunately, though various experimental ventures were launched, they tended to founder because of their expensiveness, the inexperience of their promoters and managers, and the pull of familiar institutional arrangements. A novel focus on women's constraining domestic arrangements could thus easily be submerged by more conventional desires to enhance their roles as wives and mothers, whether through vocational education, protective legislation or the family wage. Servants continued to be available to women with means, and men were little reproached for their minimal part in housekeeping (Gilman 1903; Hayden 1981; Mappen 1985; Vicinus 1985; Dyhouse 1989).

As we have seen in Chapters 2 and 3, middle-class English feminists, cautiously followed by their American sisters, also attempted to counteract charges that they had nothing to offer poorer women by founding cross-class organizations with social, educational, welfare and economic objectives. The efforts of these groups constituted one of the bolder features of the English and American women's movements before the First World War. Through them, working-class women acquired reforming and leadership experience, and were drawn into both mixed and all-female trade unions. Through them, activists from both classes proved themselves versatile campaigners. They gathered information about the circumstances of working women in and outside the home, and pressed for protective legislation and an end to sweated labour. They made a case for improved pay, hours and facilities for women, and denounced the employment of children. And seeing the link between economic and political gains, they backed strikes by women while working for female suffrage and involvement in public life. To these ends, they co-operated with sympathetic employers, politicians and factory inspectors, and with the labour movements of their two countries.

Such willingness to collaborate was essential: acting alone, women could not hope to destroy the exploitative conditions they encountered in the paid workforce. Yet there was no possibility of a comfortable relationship with non-feminists. The independence of the cross-class groups and the motives of their middle-class activists aroused the suspicion of working-class men, and even a formal link between the two could carry dangers. Whereas the American

Women's Trade Union League was not affiliated to the American Federation of Labor, its British counterpart was linked to the powerful Trades Union Congress; however, as one TUC man explained in 1915, "We always think it wiser to have the women with us because we never know what mischief they will be up to" (WTUL of America Papers). Notwithstanding the Socialist Party's recruitment of American women, and their participation in the farmers' protest alliances of the late nineteenth century, class-based movements failed to provide a secure base for feminism in the United States. In labour organizations, women found "that they must constantly look after their own interests" (Elizabeth B. Harbert Papers), while self-consciously cross-class associations had a struggle to make headway. Although the Women's Trade Union League and the Consumers' League continued their activities during the interwar years of the twentieth century, at a time when Labour women were being weaned away from their middle-class allies by the Labour Party, they were a diminished force in terms of members and funds. It did not help that, on each side of the Atlantic, working-class and middle-class women tended to have different attitudes to work beyond the home. For poorer women it could simply be an additional burden rather than a coveted means of self-realization.

None the less, the drive to bridge the class divide rightly recognized that women of all classes were restricted by a culture that elevated the private home and separate spheres for the sexes. The radical English suffragist, Hannah Mitchell, vividly recalled the pressures on working-class women to stick to their traditional duties. Public disapproval could, she felt, be "faced and borne"; but "domestic unhappiness, the price many of us paid for our opinions and activities, was a very bitter thing" (quoted in Liddington & Norris 1978). And despite their problems, English and American cross-class ventures contributed to the realization of practical gains. Working conditions were improved, child labour reduced, and protective legislation achieved (from the 1840s in Britain, from the late nineteenth century in the United States, where the laws encountered considerable economic and judicial opposition). It is difficult to see how, in the situations that faced them, feminists could have done otherwise than opt for the reformer's customary oscillation between earnest exhortation and reliance on the law (Boone 1942; Jacoby 1975; Wertheimer 1977; Soldon 1978; Tax 1979; Dye 1980; Buhle 1981; Kessler-

Harris 1982; Eisenstein 1983; Gaffin & Thoms 1983; Newton, Ryan & Walkowitz 1983; Drake 1984; John 1984; Mappen 1985; Pennington & Westover 1985; Lehrer 1987; Levine 1987, 1990; McFeely 1988; Dyhouse 1989; Leach 1989; Rose 1992; Bolt 1993).

Politics

Feminist endeavours to enter the political realm deserve the attention they have attracted, though we now acknowledge that the focus of English and American activists was not narrowly political. It is the realm where women were least welcome and where feminists achieved their clearest victories after their longest, largest, most elaborate, and ultimately most radical campaigns. In fighting for the vote, women in the two countries achieved their most pronounced degree of friendly rivalry and their most extensive personal links. Because the consequences of female enfranchisement were less dramatic than either activists or their opponents had predicted, it is possible now to disparage the achievements of the suffragists, especially since they made their final breakthrough when the enfranchisement of women no longer seemed an outlandish step. But it should not be forgotten that women had to battle to the end for their political rights, because while they could be confined to a subordinate status in the paid workforce, as voters they would be on equal terms with men. Suffragist struggles must also be understood in the context of the fierce nineteenth-century debate about the meaning of citizenship and the role of the franchise in defining it: a debate that reflected the impact of evolving liberal and radical ideology, and the attempts of a number of outsider groups to achieve independence and public recognition.

The political experiences of English and American feminists had much in common. After all, by the 1870s the political differences between England and the United States had so diminished that Mrs Fawcett felt able to assert that "the representative principle and the principles of democracy" were stronger there than anywhere else in the world (*Women's Suffrage Journal*, XV, 1884). Many women in each country came to suffragism from a reform apprenticeship, and their confidence was further encouraged by hopes of moving swiftly towards their goal in the 1860s through an alliance with a

85

disfranchised group of men. These hopes proved misplaced and, if activists were from the outset willing to employ a variety of tactics, they were frustrated in the 1860s and 1870s when they tried to assert their right to vote by going to the polls and the courts, and disappointed by the consequences of securing arrangements with the national legislatures in the 1880s for the regular consideration of women's suffrage. On neither side of the Atlantic was a major party persuaded to make it a party issue, while the support of such third parties as the Progressives in America and Labour in Britain was of little legislative value to the suffragists and alarmed conservatives. Furthermore, the loose association of suffragism with Liberals in Britain and Republicans in the United States meant that Conservatives and Democrats would not be easy to win over, and negated feminists' officially non-partisan stance.

On both sides of the Atlantic, success finally came after an era of reform had increased support for the suffragists and a world war had created political opportunities that they had effectively exploited, despite the continuing opposition of conservatives in the British House of Lords and the American Senate, and the difficulties involved in converting such initially unsympathetic leaders as the Liberal Prime Minister Herbert Asquith and the Democratic President Woodrow Wilson. Along the way, the suffrage journals of Britain and the United States monitored setbacks and achievements, while their suffrage leaders followed each other's words and worked in each other's campaigns. Hence the *History of woman suffrage* gave space to Mrs Fawcett, NAWSA conferences reported British exploits, and American activists paid tribute to British writers and raised funds for Mrs Pankhurst. American suffragists drew some of their more adventurous British allies into the international organizations that came naturally to reformers shaped by the cosmopolitan ideology of the abolitionist William Lloyd Garrison (Holton 1994b). And Americans also learned fresh tactics from their countrywomen who returned home after a British sojourn, among them Susan Anthony, Elizabeth Stanton, Harriot Blatch, Lucy Burns and Alice Paul. Similarly, British activists welcomed American visitors as speakers, planners and protesters, with Charlotte Gilman preaching her brand of socialist feminism in the company of Labour women, the sculptor Alice Morgan being gaoled for her militant activities, and Elizabeth Robins, an American actress and novelist, becoming president of the Women Writers Suffrage League in 1908, a year after she had produced her influential and uncompromisingly radical play called *Votes for women.*

In the course of their campaigns, suffragists experienced regular disagreements: the Americans in the 1860s and during the First World War, the British in the 1870s, the 1880s and during the early twentieth century. As they had initially done, these disputes reflected tensions between leaders and over strategy. Opponents used them unhelpfully, but they were unavoidable in an enterprise that drew in such diverse women and presented no obvious right course for its adherents to pursue. Suffragists had no difficulty, however, in developing a large number of arguments for the vote, claiming it as a right as well as a means by which women could influence social reform and more effective protection for the interests of women and children. And they provided the range of leaders necessary to serve the needs of the movement's large membership and the challenge of changing times.

There were, none the less, differences between British and American suffragism that reflected their different social contexts. The British campaigners, accustomed to reform endeavours that elevated men or mobilized both sexes, did not, until the last stages of their struggle, display the NAWSA leadership's caution about the role of male suffragists: a caution prompted by the conviction that men "cannot make women's disfranchisement hurt them, as it hurts us, hence cannot be our guides and ultimate appeals, as to principles and policies of action" (Elizabeth B. Harbert Papers). In several other instances they demonstrated a pragmatism that came less naturally to American activists, ever conscious of their democratic tradition. Thus from the 1880s English feminists acquired what political experience they could, and tried to advance suffragism in the process, by doing unpaid chores for the Conservative and Liberal parties (Walker 1987). Outside the radical Women's Franchise League (1889), they mainly aimed at suffrage on the same terms as men, thereby excluding propertyless single women and married women affected by the doctrine of coverture. And when a national breakthrough eluded them, they took advantage of the openings they had sought in local government. These openings became available after single women ratepayers received the municipal franchise in 1869, and women were allowed to vote for and serve on school boards (1870–1902), as poor law guardians (from 1875), on parish councils and rural district councils (regardless of marital status, from 1894), and on borough and county councils (from 1907). In America, states increasingly gave women the right to vote and become members of school boards, and to vote on questions submitted to taxpayers, while the municipal franchise was likewise extended in response to diverse pressures. But American suffragists frequently felt that such gains undermined their goal of equality with men and would benefit only elite women. English activists, operating in a system that denied the parliamentary franchise to many men, were happy to take what they could and work for more.

As far as the political systems of the two countries are concerned, the British suffragists had the advantage of needing only to convert a single legislature, while Americans hesitated over whether to seek enfranchisement state by state or through a constitutional amendment requiring action by Congress and the states. It was finally recognized that both approaches were necessary; and though they took time, it was inspiring to have won full female suffrage in eleven states by the First World War, when the last big push for the vote began. Yet most of these victories had been secured in the West, and the factors that had made for victory there – notably the desire to attract or elevate women in a region where they were scarce – either were not exportable to areas that opposed women's suffrage, or were conservative in their implications. In other words, while westerners conventionally prided themselves on their free and democratic ways, women electors were valued as a conservative or civilizing influence in wild parts, rather than as men's political equals (Grimes 1972).

The most striking contrast between British and American suffragism in its final phase was in the deployment of militant tactics (see Ch. 3). During the first two decades of the twentieth century, much-needed fresh thinking and methods were brought to the National American Woman Suffrage Association by the Congressional Union (later Woman's Party 1913), and to the National Union of Women's Suffrage Societies both by the Women's Social and Political Union and by radicals within its own and WSPU ranks who agitated for closer links with the Labour Party. But before women over thirty years of age had been enfranchised in Britain in 1918, and American women had obtained the vote through the Nineteenth Amendment in 1920, suffragists as well as their opponents had been divided over the wisdom of militancy. Although Woman's Party activists adopted it after exhausted British suffragettes had turned to more respectable war work, the widely publicized government hostility to suffragette activities was enough to deter older American feminists, wedded to persuading rather than harassing politicians. Such veterans thought that violence in particular was only "excusable in men struggling for liberty" (C. G. W. McCulloch Papers): women operated according to a superior moral code. The pacifism of the WP's Quaker members restrained American militants from imitating the WSPU's most extreme tactics, and American respect for property was so great as to make its systematic destruction an unwise resort for women. Moreover, there was a widespread recoil from a mode of protest associated with the old country when it was felt that American women were well on their way to full suffrage.

For their part, British suffragettes believed that while Americans would help them, as they had helped other freedom fighters, their distant allies might never need to resort to militancy because "we are doing the militant work for you" (Emmeline Pankhurst, quoted in Marcus 1987). The Anglo-American relationship was ever ambivalent. Yet generosity of spirit can always be found within it, and Mrs Catt spoke for many when she declared in 1908 that militancy "had awakened interest in votes for women in all quarters of the globe, and recalled the struggle of the barons in wresting the Magna Carta from King John" (*History of woman suffrage*, VI; Blackburn 1902; Fawcett 1912; Catt & Shuler 1923; Flexner 1959; Rover 1967; Stevens 1971; Morgan 1972; 1975; Paulson 1973; Raeburn 1973; Scott & Scott 1975; Pankhurst 1977; Pugh 1980; Kraditor 1981; Hume 1982; Garner 1984; Fowler 1986; Holton 1986; Lunardini 1986; Bolt 1993; Pugh 1995).

Reform

By the early twentieth century, women's role as reformers had been fully accepted in England and the United States, and they had developed an elaborate array of organizations through which, in Charlotte Gilman's words, "the woman whose range of life was wholly personal learns gradually to enter human relationships, to care for the general good, and to work for it" (Caroline Severance Papers). As we have seen, however, there was disagreement about whether activists working for the general good sufficiently advanced their own. When they came together for reform of the married women's property laws and child custody provisions, or debated divorce, birth control and abortion, the emphasis upon women's rights could not be mistaken. When women took up the improvement of urban conditions, the safeguarding of children, the protection of female sexual purity, and the securing of welfare legislation, they altered without transforming the world that men had made. In the twentieth century, after the word feminism had entered common usage and reanimated the old debate about what women wanted, those who favoured a renewal of equal rights campaigns could easily find themselves at odds with those who, supported by paternalists of all types, favoured a reaffirmation of the special interests of women. But social or maternalist feminists have been included in this study because they did improve the position of their sex, and were initially an integral and unquestioned part of the women's movements (Baker 1984; Cott 1987, 1989; Offen 1988; Black 1989; Gordon 1989, 1990, 1991; Michel & Koven 1990; Bock & Thane 1991; Skocpol 1992; Koven & Michel 1993).

The first feminists were particularly offended by the contrast between the legal and social positions of married women, and campaigns to alter the married women's property laws were under way in the United States from the 1830s, in England from the 1850s. American efforts were aided by the fact that English common law had already been modified in the young republic, and by the support of various groups for the codification and democratization of the law. It was likewise helpful that many men could see the advantage of securing women's property from dissipation by feckless spouses or destruction by the vagaries of the expansive American economy. In England, feminists were similarly assisted by reformers who wished to bring the law into line with a changing economy and polity. Activists were further encouraged by the successes of their American sisters. Yet if the state legislatures responded more readily than the British Parliament to pressures for change, so that the major gains for English women did not come until 1870 and 1882, feminists had to sustain their operations for much of the nineteenth century in each country. English and American campaigners discovered that legislators and courts might be willing to help women without abandoning their commitment to the ancient common-law doctrine of marital unity, the rock upon which family stability was alleged to rest. Feminists on both sides of the Atlantic were persuaded by their experiences in this crusade that there were many other aspects of women's legal inequality that needed to be tackled, and that women required the vote to protect themselves against unjust laws. Although frequently charged with elitism, English and American feminists pushed for working women's control of their earnings, not just for affluent women's control of their property. But there were limits to their radicalism, prudence dictating that the customary division of labour within marriage largely went unchallenged (Rabkin 1980; Basch 1982; Holcombe 1983; Poovey 1988; Leach 1989; Perkin 1989; Shanley 1989; Hoff 1991).

Divorce and parental custody rights were additional areas of concern for English and American feminists, though their experiences here were rather different. In the United States, the liberalization of divorce and the extension of women's rights regarding their children were urged as early as the 1850s by outspoken activists like Elizabeth Stanton and Susan Anthony, and divorce laws came to permit more grounds for divorce in areas where the women's movement was strong, namely New England and the West. But much was also owed to the power of the states to experiment according to local preference, to the willingness of the courts to use their discretion, and to changing attitudes to children in the nineteenth century. In England, by contrast, the two issues had to be tackled separately, progress was harder to achieve, and feminists were a factor in change over a longer period. The English infant custody law was amended in 1839 after a notable agitation by an estranged wife, Caroline Norton, and custody was extended to innocent and legally separated mothers by laws of 1873, 1878 and 1886, following feminist campaigns in which Elizabeth Wolstenholme Elmy and Frances Power Cobbe were prominent. Especially disturbed by the vulnerability of working-class women, activists involved themselves in successful drives to obtain redress from the fathers of illegitimate children (1872); to procure separation and maintenance orders (1878 and 1886); and to remove a husband's right to imprison his wife if she refused conjugal rights (1884). Yet whereas masculine chivalry could be stirred against the blatant mistreatment of women, parliament was not prepared to end men's sole guardianship of children at law and, after a breakthrough in 1857, divorce law proved elusive for over sixty years.

In 1857, a civil court for divorce and matrimonial causes was established in London. Women could sue for divorce but the expensiveness of the procedure put it beyond the reach of working-class women, whose recourse was an informal or (after 1878) legal separation. Under the law as amended in 1857, it was harder for women than men to obtain a divorce and the stigma attached to being divorced remained particularly damaging for women. Feminists who had joined lawyers and disgruntled members of the middle class in advocating a secular and simpler divorce process were disappointed with the outcome. It was not until the 1890s that they again spoke out vigorously against the unfairness and narrow grounds for divorce. It was not until 1909 that their protests contributed to the setting up of a Royal Commission on Divorce and Matrimonial Causes; and it was not until 1923 that parliament – which had been distracted by the First World War – acted on the Commission's recommendations. By the 1890s, the high incidence of divorce in America made it easier for feminists there to take up this contentious topic, at which point they directed their criticisms at the variation in state laws (McGregor 1957; Stetson 1982; Horstman 1985; Riley 1991).

Predominant among the reforms embraced by social feminists were those that concerned women's moral welfare and maternal function. The social purity movements that developed in England and America from the 1870s attacked the double standard of morality for the sexes, denounced public indecency of all kinds, raised the age of female consent for sexual activity, monitored brothel keeping, and debated the causes and consequences of prostitution without condoning its regulation by the state. In each movement, activists of a libertarian disposition found themselves at odds with individuals anxious to coerce people for their own good. The different social circumstances of the two countries none the less brought about some distinctive emphases among English and American activists. Accordingly, a strong military establishment in England had helped to produce the Contagious Diseases Acts, and the well publicized campaign to secure the laws' repeal (1869–86) made sure that they could not usefully be exported to the United States. In America, feminists were affected by their country's powerful puritan tradition and faith in the power of education, producing a radical temperance campaign, advocating sex instruction in schools, and condoning (if not always applauding) the Comstock law of 1873, which was designed to prevent the circulation of allegedly obscene materials through the mails (Pivar 1973; Rothman 1978; Walkowitz 1980, 1992; Jeffreys 1985; Mort 1987).

The Comstock law's attempt to suppress abortifacients and contraceptive materials highlights the difficulties English and American feminists encountered in tackling birth control and abortion before the interwar years of the twentieth century. Abortion had been condemned by the medical profession on both sides of the Atlantic in the light of new knowledge about how life began and because of professional misgivings about the quacks who often carried out terminations. It had been made a statutory offence in England from 1803 and from 1821 in the United States, where doctors determined to increase their standing led the drive to strengthen the state abortion laws. By the late nineteenth century, doctors and politicians were alarmed by the declining birthrate in their two countries, and saw abortion and birth control as important contributory factors in that decline. Moreover, since contraception was traditionally associated with sexual indulgence, it had little respectable support in public as long as social purity was a major force. Although a few bold feminists, socialists and advocates of population limitation did speak out on these matters, the main women's organization dealt with them very cautiously (Banks 1964; Mohr 1975; Gordon 1976; McLaren 1978; Reed 1984; Brookes 1988).

Feminist attempts to influence the passage of welfare legislation were, however, assisted by the ideas and supporters of the social purity coalition. From the 1890s, a wide range of American women drawn from clubs, settlement houses, cross-class organizations, purity groups and the federal Children's Bureau played a key part in securing protective labour legislation, widows' and mothers' pensions, the employment of matrons at police stations, municipal vice commissions, child protection agencies, and bodies to assist migrants and immigrants. A comparable array of English activists worked for a succession of children's acts, school meals and medical inspections, maternity insurance, the establishment of special schools and reformatories, and the improvement of the workplace. Such endeavours were fostered by periods of reform – Progressivism in America, a liberal resurgence in Britain – when male campaigners of many kinds accepted the need to extend the powers of the state, both to ameliorate the social and political problems created by urbanization and industrialization, and to undermine the attractions of socialism. And on both sides of the Atlantic women were well placed to influence change, given their long acquaintance with the findings of the social sciences, religious zeal, vast practical experience of social activism, and increasing politicization.

As one would expect, there were also differences between English and American social feminists at this time. In the United States, the peculiarly strong attachment to limited government, the weakness of organized labour and the unwillingness to propose class legislation had hampered the development of the welfare state, so that middle-class women, operating through their own organizations, had a unique opportunity to shape its emergence (Sklar 1985, 1993). In England, women did work through independent feminist groups but were increasingly active in labour and party organizations, more candid about class, less easy to identify as procurers of welfare measures, and able to appeal to a somewhat more assertive state (Thane 1993).

Equally understandably, there were disadvantages as well as benefits in the maternalist thrust of the women's movements. American and English working women undoubtedly gained practical assistance and links with their middle-class sisters from the feminist campaigns. On the other hand, maternalist objectives divided feminists and protected rather than empowered working-class women. Activists' proposals were often blocked or pared down by male politicians who took a more conservative view of women's social role, and the caution of such men and of powerful courts was particularly effective in the United States, notwithstanding the strength of its women reformers and their place within government via state labour bureaux and the federal Children's Bureau: a place not enjoyed by English feminists. As a result, the divisions between women because of class and race were only partly challenged by social feminism (Baker 1984; Dwork 1987; Lehrer 1987; Pleck 1987; Fitzpatrick 1990; Gordon 1990, 1991; Koven & Michel 1990; Pedersen 1990; Frankel & Dye 1991; Lewis 1991b; Muncy 1991; Scott 1991; Skocpol 1992; Thomas 1992; Boris 1993; Schneider & Schneider 1993; Thane 1993; Sklar 1995).

CHAPTER SIX

Conclusion: feminism in the interwar years

The women's movements of England and America were once seen as being in unambiguous decline between the two world wars. Having amended the marriage laws, achieved recognition as reformers, gained access to education at every level, made considerable gains in the paid workforce and secured the vote, activists were then alleged to have wound down. According to Ida Tarbell, by 1924 women were falling back on "old things, on education, discipline, character, hard thinking, hard labor. There lies the regeneration of things; not in conferences, elections, resolutions, legislation" (Ida B. Tarbell Papers). The enduring legacy of the first phase of feminism is now acknowledged, however, and the interwar years emerge as a complex period of growth as well as disappointment for women campaigners.

Looking first at gains, women in both countries formed new organizations and successfully used their existing associations to educate and mobilize the newly enfranchised female voters. Politicians were anxious to draw them more firmly into the established political parties and, fearing that they might vote as a bloc, were initially responsive to feminist pressures for new legislation to benefit women and children. In the United States, for example, activists helped to secure the establishment of the Women's Bureau; the passage of the Cable Act (1922), giving women independent citizenship; and the Sheppard-Towner Act of 1921–9, through which federal funds went to states for programmes designed to advise pregnant mothers and reduce infant mortality. At the state level, women worked effectively for measures concerning public health, wages and hours, the legal rights of women, and more efficient government. In England between 1918 and 1926, feminists were rewarded by legislation that permitted women to enter the legal profession and home civil service, sit on juries, serve as justices of the peace and police officers, draw widows' pensions if they had the care of dependent children, and receive equal treatment with men regarding the terms for divorce, rights in intestacy cases and the guardianship of children (Lemons 1973; Strachey 1978).

Women also gained during the interwar years from the provision of birth control facilities and more relaxed attitudes to manners and morals, especially in urban, middle-class circles. Victorian attitudes to sexuality, already challenged by radicals and sexologists before 1914, were further eroded by the democratizing experiences of the war (Greenwald 1980; Braybon 1981; Steinson 1982; Winter 1985; Holton 1986; Summers 1988; Pederson 1990). Those experiences had the additional effect of spreading concern for the frequent sickness and poverty of working-class women with large families beyond socialist circles. As a result, two dedicated birth controllers – Marie Stopes in England and Margaret Sanger in America – were able to lead a drive to provide clinics that would facilitate planned parenthood, particularly among the poor (Kennedy 1970; Hall 1978; Chesler 1992). In the hedonistic and turbulent 1920s, there was even some indulgence for "flappers", feminist bohemians and women lodgers: reincarnations of the "new woman", whose emancipated appearance and search for personal fulfilment no longer seemed so threatening to the social fabric (Melosh 1993).

The international endeavours of feminism likewise received an important stimulus from the First World War and its aftermath. Such endeavours had been sustained since the 1880s by women's resentment over disfranchisement, interest in the larger implications of their domestic roles, and maternal hostility to warfare. During the world conflict, many internationally minded English and American women demonstrated their willingness to put national concerns before their larger vision by undertaking or condoning war work. They were therefore not distracted by the need to defend their patriotism and were well placed to exploit the hopes for a new international order created by the founding of the League of Nations (1919). In the years that followed they lobbied the League on behalf of women's suffrage, independent nationality rights for women, the abolition of prostitution, labour legislation and peace. They won the representation of women in the League to secure these objectives, and when appealing to male members of the association made greatest headway when they emphasized social issues and the special characteristics and needs of women. Although the United States was formally outside the League, American feminists were so committed to internationalism that they were able to survive the domestic denunciation of their activities by right-wingers and play a significant part in the naval disarmament campaign; the pressure for the Kellogg-Briand anti-war treaty of 1928; the agitation for lower tariffs and reciprocal trade agreements; and the investigation of the munitions industry's role in the First World War. And in England and America, women worked for peace both with men and in their own organizations (Detzer 1948; Bussey & Tims 1965; Becker 1981; Alberti 1989; Alonso 1989, 1993; Young 1989; Miller 1992; Pugh 1992; Bacon 1993; Jeffreys-Jones 1995).

Yet English and American feminists alike experienced setbacks and some disillusionment once the euphoria of winning the vote had dissipated. Women's war work had been seen as temporary, and as the *Southampton Times* put it in 1919, "Women who left domestic service to enter the factory are now required to return to the pots and pans." To drive home the message, one factory worker recalled, "We were all stopped, just like that, no redundancy, nothing" (quoted in Griffiths 1991). Feminists sympathized with the war workers' loss of freedom, prestige and income, and renewed their protests against the poor pay and conditions of working women. But as the world struggled under the impact of economic dislocation, unwise expansion and ultimately depression, a period of political reaction set in that undermined the pre-war tilt towards social justice and secularization, and strengthened conventional notions about home and motherhood. By the mid-1920s, politicians on both sides of the Atlantic were inclined to think they had done enough for women, whose slowness to come forward as candidates for office or to vote as a bloc strengthened such complacency. There were only 36 women members of parliament between the wars, while in America only 28 women served in Congress and two in the Senate.

As the social climate changed, generational differences between feminists in the two countries became more obvious, undermining the appeal of the old activism that relied on assertions of women's moral superiority and willingness to serve society. In consequence, causes like social purity declined in popularity and sexual, personal liberation was exalted (Jeffreys 1985; Cott 1987; Harrison 1987; Kent 1988). With no issue capable of uniting women as suffragism had done, campaigners entered into divisive exchanges about the meaning and goals of feminism. These disputes adversely affected women's activism at home and abroad and were, essentially, a new version of the old debate about whether feminists should stress their equality with men or difference from them. They appeared most damagingly in discussions about protective legislation for women. Worst of all, women disagreed about the connection between feminism and pacifism and were helpless when, by the late 1930s, the world once more slid towards war.

English and American feminists were, none the less, clearly affected by their own traditions and national circumstances. In the United States, activists in the established trade union and consumer leagues, together with those in the newly formed League of Women Voters and unifying Women's Joint Congressional Committee, continued to press for social legislation, aware that American welfare provision still lagged behind that of Britain, where much was owed to the impact of socialism, a sovereign legislature, a public less committed to *laissez-faire* politics and a more demanding involvement in the First World War. American women had great scope for action at the state and municipal level, since Progressivism was still a force there, and American prosperity during the 1920s, though neither universal nor securely based, was impressive enough to secure a high level of social spending (Gordon 1986; Scott 1991). The level of separatist associational activity among American feminists seems to have been greater than that of their sisters in England, and though the American women's clubs drew back from political involvement, the League of Women Voters has survived to the present day, whereas its British equivalent, the National Union of Societies for Equal Citizenship (NUSEC), lasted only until 1945. The politicization of British women, that continued apace between the wars, did foster the creation of a wide array of specialist lobbies focused on parliament; but it did not help to make new recruits for feminism at the grass roots, because the Conservatives, who bid most effectively for women's votes, were largely unsympathetic to the cause (Pugh 1992).

If disappointment with their gains combined with uncertainty about the best way forward surfaced on both sides of the Atlantic, American feminists often displayed their resulting divisions more openly. After all, having obtained the vote with less militancy than the English, having suffered less from the war, having long dominated most aspects of international feminism, and having always enjoyed easier divorce, better educational opportunities and greater headway in the traditionally male professions, they were less inclined to moderate the optimism they had felt in 1920. And the United States as a whole was racked with contradictions and disputes as it broke free of its rural and Puritan past. Thus while Freudianism, free love and lesbianism might be discussed more openly, the birth control campaign had to proceed very cautiously in the face of an even stronger Catholic opposition than could be mustered among the English, and the absence of the kind of support it received from well placed Labour women in England (Gordon 1976; Lewis 1980; Reed 1984; Melosh 1993; McCann 1994). It is against this general background of struggle between the forces of modernity and change that we must understand the peculiarly bitter American contest over a proposed Equal Rights Amendment, designed to secure the equality of men and women throughout the nation and the places subject to its jurisdiction (Scharf & Jensen 1983).

The Amendment was sponsored from 1923 by the National Woman's Party, whose branches also worked effectively for action by state legislatures to improve women's legal status. It was opposed by most other women's groups, who felt that equal rights should be secured by state and federal legislation; that the amendment was unobtainable; and that it threatened the needed protective labour legislation for women that had been won, with difficulty, in the Progressive era. The NWP was never popular, owing to its narrow social base, excessive preoccupation with legal rights, and imperious view of its own rectitude as the "only purely feminist movement in the world" (quoted in Becker 1981). But if it underestimated the strength of opposition to its approach and the difficulties involved in obtaining another amendment to the Constitution, the Party did recognize the importance of economic equality, helped women to enter the political arena, and secured invaluable publicity for the injustices that still affected them. Unfortunately, the NWP also took its unbending view on protective legislation abroad, where it divided feminists in such bodies as the International Alliance of Women (Lemons 1973; Becker 1981; Cott 1984; Gordon 1986).

In England, quarrels among feminists may have been restrained by their need to work together to obtain full female suffrage (1928), and by their awareness of the more unpromising social circumstances facing English reformers after the war. Yet they did emerge in 1925 to distract NUSEC members, with "new feminists", led by Eleanor Rathbone, turning away from elusive equal rights goals and agitating instead for the "endowment of motherhood" through family allowances (only achieved in 1945), and the provision of birth control advice (available with cautious government support after 1930). Two years later, NUSEC was further disturbed by the question of protective legislation: a dispute that ended in compromise even as it divided feminist and Labour women; prompted the formation of a new equal rights association, the Open Door Council; and strengthened existing bodies that favoured women's labour equality, among them the Six Point Group and the Women's Freedom League (Alberti 1989; Pugh 1992; Graves 1994).

During the 1930s, however, differences between American feminists were somewhat obscured by the great opportunity that presented itself when President Roosevelt, anxious to bring new organizations and expertise to bear on the Depression, recruited advisers from formerly neglected sections of the population. The result was that over a hundred women held prominent appointments in the New Deal. They had largely begun their careers in women's organizations, and the link between the government's proliferating agencies and women's reform networks was an empowering one for female activists. But while their impact on Democratic welfare legislation was real, it should not be exaggerated. As English women involved in party politics had discovered before them, American campaigners found that they were expected to put party priorities at the top of their agenda, and these were by no means feminist. The New Deal was committed to providing relief and recovery as much as reform, and traditional objections to women (especially married women) working were strengthened at a time of frighteningly high unemployment. Women often benefited from New Deal measures, notably the industrial codes drawn up under the National Recovery Administration (1933–5); the relief programmes initiated by the Works Progress Administration (1935); and the minimum wage protection resulting from the Fair Labor Standards Act (1938). Yet they continued to encounter discrimination in the workplace and discouragement when they stood for elective office (Chafe 1972; Scharf 1980; Ware 1981, 1982).

For English women, the 1930s provided no great political opportunity. The coalition government of the time, needing to accommodate representatives of all three major parties, offered them little prospect of office. There was no British "new deal" and feminists were unable to participate in a drive for fresh legislation that would benefit their sex. Campaigns still continued and feminist associations survived, but politicians beset by domestic and foreign challenges did not hesitate to downgrade women's issues. And feminists were not helped by the growth of Women's Institutes (after 1915) and Townswomen's Guilds (by the late 1920s). While these bodies sought to educate women as citizens and trained them for public life, they avoided the feminist label and increasingly concentrated on local, social and domestic affairs. Having been less affected than American activists by the philosophy of domesticity, English organization women felt its full impact in the 1930s (Jenkins 1953; Stott 1978; Banks 1981; Pugh 1992).

By the Second World War, feminists in England and America had produced many-faceted movements that learned from each other but were proud of their distinctive ways and achievements. In both countries they had changed the agenda of politics, forcing men to take seriously their concerns and their votes. In both countries they had collaborated with other reformers, challenged conventional thinking, spread feminist ideas, organized and politicized women, enhanced their sense of worth and sisterhood, and brought about changes in the law. They had also prepared the way for future successes and debates (Bock & James 1992), and received the burdensome tribute of hostility, ridicule and concerted opposition.

Neither the English nor the American movement deserves to be seen as more radical or more effective than the other. Organized activism began in the United States and the separate associations of American feminism, necessitated by its federal structure and encouraged by its assertive courts, were particularly strong. However, the English were initially more successful in securing the passage of social purity and welfare legislation, candidly confronting class questions, willingly involving themselves in political parties, and exploiting the advantage of being able to obtain national legislation from a legislature less committed to *laissez-faire* than its American counterpart. English and American feminists are comparable in that their achievements outweigh their disappointments. Yet those disappointments are considerable. In neither country were feminists able to win the endorsement of the majority of women, to resolve their ideological inconsistencies, or to prevent the quarrels that undermined their movements. Mobilizing for specific ends always proved easier than sustaining umbrella associations, just as pressing for the objectives of social feminism proved easier but riskier than pushing for equal rights. Activists in the two countries failed to persuade men to accept them as their political and economic equals, failed to redress the unequal sexual division of labour within marriage, and abandoned militant tactics very quickly after they had been adopted within the suffrage campaign. Women in the 1930s generally remained as anxious to please and uneasy about alienating male opinion as they had been in the 1870s.

Select bibliography

Addams, J. (ed.). *Twenty years at Hull House.* New York: Signet Classic, New American Library, 1981. Originally published 1910.

Alaya, F. Victorian science and the "genius" of women. *Journal of the History of Ideas* 38, 1977.

Alberti, J. *Beyond suffrage: feminists in war and peace, 1914–1928.* London: Macmillan, 1989.

Alexander, S. (ed.). *Women's Fabian tracts.* London and New York: Routledge, 1988.

Alonso, H. H. *The Women's Peace Union and the outlawing of war, 1921–1942.* Knoxville: University of Tennessee Press, 1989.

— *Peace as a women's issue: a history of the U.S. movement for world peace and women's rights.* Syracuse, NY: Syracuse University Press, 1993.

Ammons, E. *Conflicting stories: American women writers at the turn into the twentieth century.* New York: Oxford University Press, 1991.

Atkinson, P. Fitness, feminism and schooling. In *The nineteenth century woman: her cultural and physical world*, S. Delamont & L. Duffin (eds). London: Croom Helm; New York: Barnes & Noble, 1978.

Avery, G. *The best type of girl: a history of girls' independent schools.* London: André Deutsch, 1991.

Bacon, M. *One woman's passion for peace and freedom: the life of Mildred Scott Olmstead.* Syracuse, NY: Syracuse University Press, 1993.

Bagwell, P. S. & G. E. Mingay. *Britain and America: a study of economic change, 1850–1939.* London: Routledge & Kegan Paul, 1970.

Baker, P. The domestication of politics: women and American political society, 1780–1920. *American Historical Review* 89, 1984.

Ballhatchet, K. *Race, sex and class under the Raj: imperial attitudes and policies and their critics, 1793–1905.* London: Weidenfeld & Nicolson, 1980.

Baly, M. *Florence Nightingale and the nursing legacy*. London: Routledge, 1988.

Banks, J. A. & O. Banks. *Feminism and family planning in Victorian England*. New York: Schocken Books; Liverpool: Liverpool University Press, 1964.

Banks, O. *Faces of feminism: a study of feminism as a social movement*. Oxford: Martin Robertson, 1981.

— *Becoming a feminist: the social origins of "first wave" feminism*. Brighton: Wheatsheaf, 1986.

Barr, P. *The memsahibs: the women of Victorian England*. London: Secker & Warburg, 1976.

Basch, N. *In the eyes of the law: women, marriage and property in nineteenth century New York*. Ithaca, NY: Cornell University Press, 1982.

Becker, S. D. *The origins of the Equal Rights Amendment: American feminism between the Wars*. Westport, Conn. and London: Greenwood Press, 1981.

Bederman, G. *Manliness and civilization: a cultural history of gender and race in the United States, 1880–1917*. Chicago: Chicago University Press, 1995.

Bell, E. M. *Storming the citadel: the rise of the woman doctor*. London: Constable, 1953.

Bennett, D. *Emily Davies and the liberation of women, 1830–1921*. London: André Deutsch, 1990.

Berridge, V. & G. Edward. *Opium and the people*. London: Allen Lane, 1981.

Black, N. *Social feminism*. Ithaca, NY: Cornell University Press, 1989.

Blackburn, H. *Women's suffrage: a record of the women's suffrage movement in the British Isles*. London and Oxford: Williams & Norgate, 1902.

Bland, L. Marriage laid bare: middle-class women and marital sex, 1880s–1914. In *Labour and love: women's experience of home and family, 1850–1940*, J. Lewis (ed.). Oxford: Blackwell, 1986.

— *Banishing the beast: English feminism and sexual morality, 1885–1914*. Harmondsworth: Penguin, 1995.

Bliss, B. Militancy: the insurrection that failed. *Contemporary Review* **201**, 1962.

Bock, G. & S. James (eds). *Beyond equality and difference: citizenship, feminist politics and female subjectivity*. London: Routledge, 1992.

Bock, G. & P. Thane (eds). *Maternity and gender policies: women and the rise of European welfare states, 1880s–1950s*. London: Routledge, 1991.

Bolt, C. *Victorian attitudes to race*. London and Toronto: Routledge & Kegan Paul and University of Toronto Press, 1971.

— Race and the Victorians. In *British imperialism in the Nineteenth century*, C. C. Eldridge (ed.). London: Macmillan, 1984.

— *American Indian policy and American reform: case studies of the campaign to assimilate the American Indians*. London: Allen & Unwin, 1987.

— *The women's movements in the United States and Britain from the 1790s to the 1920s*. Hemel Hempstead: Harvester Wheatsheaf; Amherst: University of Massachusetts Press, 1993.

Bondfield, M. *A life's work*. London: Hutchinson, 1949.

Boone, G. *The Women's Trade Union League in Great Britain and the United States of America*. New York: Columbia University Press, 1942.

Boris, E. The power of motherhood: black and white women redefine the political. In *Mothers of a new world: maternalist politics and the origins of welfare states*, S. Koven & S. Michel (eds). London: Routledge, 1993.

Bosch, M. with A. Kloosterman (eds). *Politics and friendship: letters from the International Woman Suffrage Alliance, 1902–1942*. Columbus, Ohio: Ohio State University Press, 1990.

Boyd, N. *Josephine Butler, Octavia Hill, Florence Nightingale: three Victorian women who changed their world*. London: Macmillan, 1982.

Braybon, G. *Women workers in the First World War*. London: Croom Helm, 1981.

Brittain, V. *Pethick-Lawrence: a portrait*. London: George Allen & Unwin, 1963.

Brod, H. (ed.). *The making of masculinities*. Boston: Allen & Unwin, 1987.

Brookes, B. *Abortion in England, 1900–1967*. London: Croom Helm, 1988.

Brown, E. B. Womanist consciousness: Maggie Lena Walker and the Independent Order of Saint Luke. In *Unequal sisters: a multi-cultural reader in U.S. women's history*, V. L. Ruiz & E. C. DuBois (eds). New York and London: Routledge, 1990.

Bryant, M. *The unexpected revolution: a study of the history of the education of women and girls in the nineteenth century*. London: NFER Publishing, University of London, Institute of Education, 1979.

Bryce, J. *The American commonwealth* [2 vols]. London: Macmillan, 1889.

Buechler, S. M. *The transformation of the woman suffrage movement: the case of Illinois 1850–1920*. New Brunswick, NJ: Rutgers University Press, 1986.

— *Women's movements in the United States*. New Brunswick and London: Rutgers University Press, 1990.

Buhle, M. J. *Women and American socialism, 1870–1920*. Urbana: University of Illinois Press, 1981.

Burstyn, J. N. *Victorian education and the ideal of womanhood*. London: Croom Helm; Totowa, NJ: Barnes & Noble, 1980.

Burton, A. *Burdens of history: British feminists, Indian women and imperial culture, 1865–1915*. Chapel Hill, NC: University of North Carolina Press, 1994.

Burton, A. M. British feminists and the Indian woman, 1865–1915. *Women's Studies International Forum* 13, 1990.

Bussey, G. & M. Tims. *The Women's International League for Peace and Freedom, 1915–1965*. London: Allen & Unwin, 1965.

Caine, B. *Victorian feminists*. Oxford: Oxford University Press, 1992.

Callaway, H. *Gender, culture and empire: European women in colonial Nigeria*. Urbana: University of Illinois Press, 1987.

Camhi, J. J. *Women against women: American anti-suffragism, 1880–1920*. New York: Carlson, 1994.

Catt, C. C. & N. R. Shuler. *Woman suffrage and politics: the inner story of the suffrage movement*. New York: Charles Scribner's Sons, 1923.

Chafe, W. H. *The American woman: her changing social, economic and political roles, 1920–1970*. New York: Oxford University Press, 1972.

Chambers-Schiller, L. *Liberty a better husband: single women in America, the generations of 1780–1840*. New Haven and London: Yale University Press, 1984.

Chaudhuri, N. & M. Strobel (eds). *Western women and imperialism*. Bloomington: Indiana University Press, 1992.

Chesler, E. *Woman of valor: Margaret Sanger and the birth control movement in America*. New York: Summit Books, 1992.

Chinn, C. *They worked all their lives*. Manchester: Manchester University Press, 1988.

Christ, C. Victorian masculinity and the angel in the house. In *A widening sphere: changing roles of Victorian women*, M. Vicinus (ed.). London: Methuen, 1980.

Cobbe, F. P. *The Life of Frances Power Cobbe* [2 vols]. London: R. Bentley, 1904.

Collette, C. *For labour and for women: the Women's Labour League, 1906–1918*. Manchester: Manchester University Press, 1989.

Colley, L. *Britons: forging the nation, 1707–1837*. London: Pimlico, 1992.

Conway, J. Stereotypes of femininity in a theory of sexual evolution. In *Suffer and be still: women in the Victorian era*, M. Vicinus (ed.). London: Methuen, 1980.

Cook, B. W. *Eleanor Roosevelt, 1884–1933*. New York: Viking, 1992.

Coslett, T. *Woman to woman: female friendship in Victorian fiction*. Atlantic Highlands, NJ: Humanities Press, 1988.

Cott, N. Feminist politics in the 1920s: the National Woman's Party. *Journal of American History* 71, 1984.

— *The grounding of modern feminism*. New Haven, Conn. and London: Yale University Press, 1987.

— What's in a name? The limits of "social feminism", or, expanding the vocabulary of women's history. *Journal of American History* 76, 1989.

Davis, A. *Women, race and class*. New York: Random House, 1981.

106

Degler, C. *At odds: women and the family in America from the Revolution to the present*. New York: Oxford University Press, 1980.

Delamont, S. The contradictions in ladies' education. In *The nineteenth century woman: her cultural and physical world*, S. Delamont & L. Duffin (eds). London: Croom Helm; New York: Barnes & Noble, 1978.

Dennis, P. *The autobiography of an American Communist: a personal view of a political life, 1925–1975*. Westport, Conn.: Lawrence Hill, 1977.

Detzer, D. *Appointment on the Hill*. New York: H. Holt, 1948.

Drake, B. *Women in trade unions*. London: Virago, 1984. Originally published 1920.

DuBois, E. C. *Feminism and suffrage: the emergence of an independent women's movement in America, 1848–1868*. Ithaca, NY: Cornell University Press, 1978.

— Working women, class relations, and suffrage militance: Harriot Stanton Blatch and the New York woman suffrage movement, 1844–1909. *Journal of American History* 74, 1987.

Dwork, D. *War is good for babies and other young children: a history of the infant and child welfare movement in England, 1898–1918*. London: Tavistock, 1987.

Dye, N. S. *As equals and as sisters: feminism, the labor movement and the Women's Trade Union League of New York*. Columbia: University of Missouri Press, 1980.

Dyhouse, C. *Girls growing up in late Victorian and Edwardian England*. London: Routledge & Kegan Paul, 1981.

— *Feminism and the family in England, 1880–1939*. Oxford: Basil Blackwell, 1989.

Eisenstein, S. *Give us bread but give us roses: working women's consciousness in the United States, 1890 to the First World War*. London: Routledge & Kegan Paul, 1983.

Ellsworth, E. W. *Liberators of the female mind: the Shirreff sisters, educational reform and the women's movement*. Westport, Conn.: Greenwood Press, 1979.

Engels, F. *Origin of the family, private property and the state* [2 vols]. New York: Octagon Books, 1966. Originally published 1884.

Evans, R. J. *The feminists: women's emancipation movements in Europe, America and Australasia, 1840–1920*. London and Totowa, NJ: Croom Helm, 1977.

Faderman, L. *Surpassing the love of men*. New York: William Morrow, 1981.

Fawcett, M. G. *Women's suffrage: a short history of a great movement*. London: Jack, 1912.

— *What I remember*. London: T. Fisher Unwin, 1924.

First, R. & A. Scott. *Olive Schreiner*. New York: Schocken Books, 1980.

Fitzgerald, T. A. *The National Council of Negro Women and the feminist movement*. Georgetown: Georgetown University Press, 1985.

Fitzpatrick, E. *Endless crusade: women social scientists and Progressive reform*. New York: Oxford University Press, 1990.

Fletcher, S. *Feminists and bureaucrats: a study in the development of girls' education in the nineteenth century*. Cambridge: Cambridge University Press, 1980.

Flexner, E. *Century of struggle: the woman's rights movement in the United States*. Cambridge, Mass.: Belknap Press of Harvard University Press, 1959.

Flint, K. *The woman reader, 1837–1914*. Oxford: Oxford University Press, 1993.

Forster, M. *Significant sisters: the grassroots of active feminism, 1839–1939*. Harmondsworth: Penguin, 1986.

Foster, C. *Women for all seasons: the story of the Women's International League for Peace and Freedom*. Athens, Ga. and London: University of Georgia Press, 1989.

Fowler, R. B. *Carrie Catt: feminist politician*. Boston, Mass.: Northeastern University Press, 1986.

Fox-Genovese, E. *Within the plantation household: black and white women of the old South*. Chapel Hill and London: University of North Carolina Press, 1988.

Frankel, N. & N. S. Dye (eds). *Gender, class, race and reform in the Progressive era*. Lexington, Ky.: University Press of Kentucky, 1991.

Freedman, E. Separatism as a strategy: female institution building, 1870–1930. *Feminist Studies* 5, 1979.

Gaffin, J. & D. Thoms. *Caring and sharing: the centenary history of the Women's Co-operative Guild*. Manchester: Co-operative Union, 1983.

Gardner, V. & S. Rutherford (eds). *The new woman and her sisters: feminism and the theatre, 1850–1914*. Hemel Hempstead: Harvester Wheatsheaf, 1992.

Garner, L. *Stepping stones to women's liberty: feminist ideas in the women's suffrage movement, 1900–1919*. London: Heinemann, 1984.

Giddings, P. *When and where I enter: the impact of race and sex in America*. New York: William Morrow, 1984.

Gilman, C. *The home, its work and influence*. New York: Charlton, 1903.

— *Woman and economics: the economic factor between men and women as a factor in evolution*. New York: Harper & Row, 1966. Originally published 1898.

Ginzberg, L. D. *Women and the work of benevolence: morality, politics and class in the nineteenth-century United States*. New Haven, Conn. and London: Yale University Press, 1990.

Gluck, S. B. *From parlor to prison: five American suffragists talk about their lives.* New York: Monthly Review Press, 1985.

Goldin, C. Maximum hours legislation and female employment: a reassessment. *Journal of Political Economy* 96, 1988.

Gordon, F. *After winning: the legacy of the New Jersey suffragists, 1920–1947.* New Brunswick, NJ: Rutgers University Press, 1986.

Gordon, L. *Woman's body, woman's right: a social history of birth control in America.* Harmondsworth: Penguin, 1976.

— *Heroes of their own lives: the politics and history of family violence.* London: Virago, 1989.

— (ed.) *Women, the state and welfare.* Madison: University of Wisconsin Press, 1990.

— Black and white visions of welfare: women's welfare activism, 1890–1945. *Journal of American History* 78, 1991.

Graham, P. A. Expansion and exclusion: a history of women in American higher education. *Signs* 3, 1978.

Graves, P. M. *Labour women: women in British working-class politics, 1918–1939.* Cambridge: Cambridge University Press, 1994.

Greenwald, M. W. *Women, war, and work: the impact of World War I on women workers in the United States.* Westport, Conn. and London: Greenwood Press, 1980.

Griffin, C. S. *The ferment of reform, 1830–1860.* New York: Thomas Y. Cromwell, 1967.

Griffith, E. *In her own right: the life of Elizabeth Cady Stanton.* New York: Oxford University Press, 1984.

Griffiths, G. *Women's factory work in World War I.* Stroud: Allen Sutton, 1991.

Grimes, A. *The Puritan ethic and woman suffrage.* New York: Oxford University Press, 1972.

Guarneri, C. J. *The utopian alternative: Fourierism in nineteenth-century America.* Ithaca: Cornell University Press, 1991.

Hale, T. F. F. W. Pethick Lawrence and the suffragettes. *Contemporary Review* 225, 1974.

Hall, J. D. *Revolt against chivalry: Jessie Daniel Ames and the women's campaign against lynching.* New York: Columbia University Press, 1979.

Hall, R. *Marie Stopes: a biography.* London: Virago Press, 1978.

Haller, J. S. & R. M. Haller. *The physician and sexuality in Victorian America.* Urbana: University of Illinois Press, 1974.

Hammerton, A.J. *Emigrant gentlewomen: genteel poverty and female emigration, 1830–1914.* London and Totowa, NJ: Croom Helm, 1979.

Harper, I. H. *The life and work of Susan B. Anthony* [3 vols]. Salem, NH: Ayer Company, 1983. Originally published 1898.

Harrison, B. *Separate spheres: the opposition to women's suffrage in Britain.* London: Croom Helm, 1978.

— A genealogy of reform in modern Britain. In *Anti-slavery, religion, and reform: essays in memory of Roger Anstey*, C. Bolt & S. Drescher (eds). Folkestone: Dawson; Hamden, Conn.: Archon, 1980.

— Women's health and the women's movement in Britain, 1840–1940. In *Biology, medicine and society, 1840–1940*, C. Webster (ed.). Cambridge: Cambridge University Press, 1981.

— The act of militancy: violence and the suffragettes, 1904–1914. In *Peaceable kingdom: stability and change in modern Britain*, B. Harrison (ed.). Oxford: Oxford University Press, 1982.

— *Prudent revolutionaries: portraits of British feminists between the Wars.* Oxford: Oxford University Press, 1987.

— Class and gender in modern British labour history. *Past and Present* **124**, 1989.

Hayden, D. *The grand domestic revolution: a history of feminist designs for American homes, neighbourhoods and cities.* Cambridge, Mass.: MIT Press, 1982.

Helsinger, E. K., R. L. Sheets, W. Veeder. *The woman question: society and Literature in Britain and America, 1837–1883* vol. 3 of a trilogy. New York and London: Garland Publishing, 1983.

Hersh, B. G. *The slavery of sex: feminist-abolitionists in America.* Urbana: University of Illinois Press, 1978.

Higginbotham, E. B. *Righteous discontent: the women's movement in the Baptist church, 1880–1920.* Cambridge, Mass.: Harvard University Press, 1993.

Hine, D. C. *When the truth is told: a history of black women's culture and community in Indiana, 1875–1950.* Indianapolis, Ind.: National Council of Negro Women, 1981.

— *Hine sight: black women and the reconstruction of American history.* New York: Carlson, 1995.

Hoff, J. *Law, gender and injustice: a legal history of U.S. women.* New York: New York University Press, 1991.

Holcombe, L. *Victorian ladies at work: middle class working women in England and Wales, 1850–1914.* Newton Abbot: David & Charles, 1973.

— *Wives and property: reform of the married women's property law in nineteenth century England.* Toronto: University of Toronto Press, 1983.

Hollis, P. *Ladies elect: women in English local government, 1865–1914.* Oxford: Oxford University Press, 1987.

Holt, R. *Mary McLeod Bethune.* Garden City, NY: Doubleday, 1964.

Holton, S. S. *Feminism and democracy: women's suffrage and reform politics in Britain, 1900–1918.* Cambridge: Cambridge University Press, 1986.

— Free love and Victorian feminism: the divers matrimonials of Elizabeth Wolstenholme and Ben Elmy. *Victorian Studies* **137**, 1994a.

110

— "To educate women into rebellion": Elizabeth Cady Stanton and the creation of a transatlantic network of radical suffragists. *American Historical Review* 99, 1994b.

hooks, b. *Ain't I a woman: black women and feminism*. Boston: South End Press, 1981.

Horowitz, H. L. *Alma mater: design and experience in the women's colleges from their 19th century beginnings to the 1930s*. New York: Knopf, 1984.

Horsman, R. *Race and manifest destiny: the origins of American racial Anglo-Saxonism*. Cambridge, Mass.: Harvard University Press, 1981.

Horstman, A. *Victorian divorce*. New York, Conn. and London: Yale University Press, 1987.

Hull, G. T. et al. (eds). *All the women are white, all the blacks are men but some of us are brave: black women's studies*. Old Westbury, NY: Feminist Press, 1982.

Hume, L. *The National Union of Women's Suffrage Societies, 1897–1914*. New York and London: Garland Publishing, 1982.

Hunter, J. *The gospel of gentility: American women missionaries in turn-of-the-century China*. New Haven and London: Yale University Press, 1984.

Hurwitz, E. F. The international sisterhood. In *Becoming visible: women in European history*, R. Bridenthal, C. Koonz & S. Stuard (eds). Boston: Houghton Mifflin, 1977.

Hyam, R. *Empire and sexuality: the British experience*. Manchester: Manchester University Press, 1990.

Jablonsky, T. T. *The home, heaven, and mother party: female anti-suffragists in the United States, 1868–1920*. New York: Carlson, 1994.

Jacoby, R. M. The Women's Trade Union League and American feminism. *Feminist Studies* 2, 1975.

Janiewski, D. E. *Sisterhood denied: race, gender and class in a New South community*. Philadelphia: Temple University, 1985.

Jeffreys, S. *The spinster and her enemies: feminism and sexuality, 1880–1930*. London and New York: Pandora, 1985.

Jeffreys-Jones, R. *Changing differences: women and the shaping of American foreign policy*. New Brunswick, NJ: Rutgers University Press, 1995.

John, A. *By the sweat of their brow: women workers at Victorian coal mines*. London: Routledge & Kegan Paul, 1984.

— *Elizabeth Robins: staging a life, 1862–1952*. London: Routledge, 1995.

Jones, J. *Labor of love, labor of sorrow: black women, work and the family from slavery to the present*. New York: Vintage Books, 1985.

Kennedy, D. *Birth control in America: the career of Margaret Sanger*. New Haven, Conn.: Yale University Press, 1970.

Kent, S. K. The politics of sexual difference: World War I and the decline of British feminism. *Journal of British Studies* 27, 1988.

— *Sex and suffrage in Britain, 1860–1914*. London: Routledge, 1990.

Kessler-Harris, A. *Out to work: a history of wage-earning women in the United States.* Oxford: Oxford University Press, 1982.

Kimmel, M. S. (ed.). *Changing men: new directions in research on men and masculinity.* Los Angeles: Sage, 1987.

Koven, S. & S. Michel (eds). *Mothers of a new world: maternalist politics and the origins of welfare states.* London: Routledge, 1993.

Kraditor, A. *The ideas of the woman suffrage movement, 1890–1920.* New York: W. W. Norton, 1981.

Lagemann, E. C. *A generation of women: education in the lives of Progressive reformers.* Cambridge, Mass.: Harvard University Press, 1979.

Lake, M. The politics of respectability: identifying the masculinist context. *Historical Studies* 22, 1986.

Leach, W. *True love and perfect union: the feminist reform of sex and society.* Middletown, Conn.: Wesleyan University Press, 2nd edn 1989.

Lebsock, S. *The free women of Petersburg: status and culture in a southern town, 1784–1860.* New York: W. W. Norton, 1984.

Lehrer, S. *Origins of protective labor legislation for women, 1905–1925.* Albany: State University of New York Press, 1987.

Lemons, J. S. *The woman citizen: social feminism in the 1920s.* Urbana: University of Illinois Press, 1973.

Leonardi, S. L. *Dangerous by degrees: women at Oxford and the Somerville College novelists.* New Brunswick and London: Rutgers University Press, 1989.

Lerner, G. (ed.). *Black women in white America: a documentary history.* New York: Pantheon Books, 1972.

— *The creation of feminist consciousness: from the Middle Ages to Eighteen-seventy.* New York and Oxford: Oxford University Press, 1993.

L'Esperance, J. Doctors and women in nineteenth century society: sexuality and role. In *Health care and popular medicine in nineteenth century England: essays in the social history of medicine,* J. Woodward & D. Richards (eds). London: Croom Helm, 1977.

Levine, P. *Victorian feminism.* London: Hutchinson, 1987.

— *Feminist lives in Victorian England: private roles and public commitment.* Oxford: Blackwell, 1990.

Lewis, J. *The politics of motherhood: child and maternal welfare in England, 1900–1939.* London: Croom Helm; Montreal: McGill-Queen's University, 1980.

— *Women in England, 1870–1950: social divisions and social change.* Brighton: Wheatsheaf; Bloomington: Indiana University Press, 1984.

— *Women and social action in Victorian and Edwardian England.* Aldershot: Edward Elgar, 1991a.

— Models of equality for women: the case of state support for children in twentieth-century Britain. In *Maternity and gender policies: women and the rise of European welfare states, 1880s–1950s*, G. Bock & P. Thane (eds). London: Routledge, 1991b.

Liddington, J. & J. Norris. *One hand tied behind us: the rise of the women's suffrage movement*. London: Virago Press, 1978.

Lind, M. A. *The compassionate memsahibs: welfare activities of British women in India, 1900–1947*. Westport, Conn.: Greenwood Press, 1988.

Linton, E. L. The modern revolt. *Macmillan's Magazine* 23, 1870.

Loewenberg, B. & R. Bogin (eds). *Black women in nineteenth century life: their thoughts, their words, their feelings*. University Park: Pennsylvania State University Press, 1976.

Lorimer, D. *Colour, class and the Victorians: English attitudes to the Negro in the mid-nineteenth century*. Leicester: Leicester University Press, 1978.

Lunardini, A. *From equal suffrage to equal rights: Alice Paul and the National Woman's Party, 1910–1928*. New York: New York University Press, 1986.

Mackinnon, C. A. Feminism, Marxism, method and the state: an agenda for theory. In *Feminist theory: a critique of ideology*, N. O. Keohane, M. Z. Rosaldo, B. C. Gelpi (eds). Brighton: Harvester, 1982.

Mangan, J. A. & J. Walvin (eds). *Manliness and morality: middle-class masculinity in Britain and America, 1800–1940*. Manchester: Manchester University Press, 1987.

Manton, J. *Elizabeth Garrett Anderson*. London: Methuen, 1965.

Mappen, E. *Helping women at work: the Woman's Industrial Council, 1889–1914*. London: Hutchinson, 1985.

Marcus, J. (ed.) *Suffrage and the Pankhursts*. London: Routledge & Kegan Paul, 1987.

Mason, M. *The making of Victorian sexual attitudes*. Oxford: Oxford University Press, 1994.

McCann, C. *Birth control politics in the United States, 1916–1945*. Ithaca, NY: Cornell University Press, 1994.

McCrone, K. *Sport and the physical emancipation of English women, 1870–1914*. London: Routledge, 1988.

McFeely, M. D. *Lady inspectors: the campaign for a better workplace, 1893–1921*. Oxford: Basil Blackwell, 1988.

McGregor, O. R. *Divorce in England: a centenary study*. London: Heinemann, 1957.

McLaren, A. *Birth Control in nineteenth-century England*. London: Croom Helm, 1978.

McWilliams-Tullberg, R. *Women at Cambridge: a man's university – though of a mixed type*. London: Victor Gollancz, 1975.

— Women and degrees at Cambridge University, 1862–1897. In *A widening sphere: changing roles of Victorian women*, M. Vicinus (ed.). London: Methuen, 1980.

Melosh, B. (ed.) *Gender and American history since 1890.* London: Routledge, 1993.

Michel, S. & S. Koven. Womanly duties: maternalist politics and the origins of welfare states in France, Germany, Great Britain, and the United States, 1880–1920. *American Historical Review* 95, 1990.

Midgley, C. *Women Against Slavery: the British campaigns, 1780–1870.* London and New York: Routledge, 1992.

Mill, J. S. & H. T. Mill. *Essays on sex equality.* Chicago and London: University of Chicago Press, 1970. Alice S. Rossi (ed.).

Miller, C. *Lobbying the League: women's international organizations and the League of Nations.* PhD thesis. Oxford University, 1992.

Mohr, J. C. *Abortion in America: the origins and evolution of national policy, 1800–1900.* New York: Oxford University Press, 1975.

Morgan, D. *Suffragists and Democrats: the politics of woman suffrage in America.* East Lansing: Michigan State University Press, 1972.

— *Suffragists and Liberals: the politics of woman suffrage in Britain.* Oxford: Basil Blackwell, 1975.

Morgan, D. H. J. *Discovering men.* London and New York: Routledge, 1992.

Morley, A. & S. Stanley. *The life and death of Emily Wilding Davison.* London: The Women's Press, 1988.

Mort, F. *Dangerous sexualities: medico-moral politics in England since 1830.* London: Routledge, 1987.

Muncy, R. *Creating a female dominion in American reform, 1890–1935.* New York: Oxford University Press, 1991.

Neverdon-Morton, C. *Afro-American women of the South and the advancement of the race, 1895–1925.* Knoxville: University of Kentucky Press, 1989.

Newton, J. L., M. P. Ryan, J. R. Walkowitz (eds). *Sex and class in women's history.* London: Routledge & Kegan Paul, 1983.

O'Neill, W. *Divorce in the Progressive era.* New Haven: Yale University Press, 1967.

— *The woman movement: feminism in the United States and England.* London: Allen & Unwin; New York: Barnes & Noble, 1969a.

— *Everyone was brave: a history of feminism in America.* New York: Quadrangle, 1969b.

Offen, K. Defining feminism: a comparative historical approach. *Signs* 14, 1988.

Pankhurst, S. *The suffragette movement.* London: Virago, 1977. Originally published 1931.

Parkes, B. *Essays on women's work.* London: Alexander Strahan, 1865.

Paulson, R. E. *Women's suffrage and prohibition: a comparative study of equality and social control.* Glenview, Ill.: Scott, Foresman, 1973.

Payne, E. *Reform, labor and feminism: Margaret Dreier Robins and the Women's Trade Union League.* Urbana: University of Illinois Press, 1988.

Pedersen, J. S. The reform of women's secondary and higher education: institutional change and social values in mid and late Victorian England. *History of Education Quarterly,* Spring, 1979.

Pederson, S. Offenders, welfare and citizenship in Britain during the Great War. *American Historical Review* 95, 1990.

Peiss, K. *Cheap amusements: working women and leisure in turn-of-the-century New York.* Philadelphia: Temple University Press, 1986.

Pennington, S. & B. Westover. *A hidden workforce: women homeworkers in Britain, 1850–1985.* London: Macmillan, 1985.

Perkin, J. *Women and marriage in nineteenth-century England.* London: Routledge, 1989.

Peterson, M. J. The Victorian governess: status incongruence in the family and society. In *Suffer and be still: women in the Victorian age,* M. Vicinus (ed.). London: Methuen, 1980.

Pethick-Lawrence, E. *My part in a changing world.* London: Victor Gollancz, 1938.

Pivar, D. J. *Purity crusade, sexual morality and social control, 1868–1900.* Westport, Conn.: Greenwood Press, 1973.

Pleck, E. *Domestic tyranny: the making of American social policy against family violence from colonial times to the present.* New York: Oxford University Press, 1987.

Pole, J. R. *The pursuit of equality in American history.* Berkeley: University of California Press, 1978.

Poovey, M. *Uneven developments: the ideological work of gender in mid-Victorian England.* Chicago: University of Chicago Press, 1988.

Prochaska, F. K. *Women and philanthropy in nineteenth-century England.* Oxford: Oxford University Press, 1980.

Pryor, E. B. *Clara Barton: professional angel.* Philadelphia: University of Pennsylvania Press, 1987.

Pugh, M. *Women's suffrage in Britain, 1867–1928.* London: Historical Association, 1980.

— *Women and the women's movement in Britain, 1914–1959.* London: Macmillan, 1992.

— *Votes for women in Britain, 1865–1928.* London: Historical Association, 1995.

Purvis, J. *A history of women's education in England, 1800–1914.* Milton Keynes: Open University Press, 1991.

Rabkin, P. A. *Fathers to daughters: the legal foundation of female emancipation.* Westport, Conn.: Greenwood Press, 1980.

Raeburn, A. *Militant suffragettes.* London: Joseph, 1973.

Ramusack, B. N. Cultural missionaries, maternal imperialists, feminist allies: British women activists in India, 1865–1945. *Women's Studies International Forum* 13, 1990.

Reed, J. *The birth control movement in American society: from private vice to public virtue.* Princeton University Press, 1984.

Rendall, J. *The origins of modern feminism: women in Britain, France and the United States 1780–1860.* London: Macmillan, 1985.

— Uneven developments: women's history, feminist history, and gender history in great Britain. In *Writing women's history: international perspectives,* K. Offen, R. R. Pierson, J. Rendall (eds). London: Macmillan, 1991.

— Citizenship, culture and civilisation: the languages of British suffragists, 1866–1874. In *Suffrage and beyond: international perspectives,* C. Daley and M. Nolan (eds.). Auckland: Auckland University Press, 1994.

Renton, A. *Tyrant or victim? A history of the British governess.* London: Weidenfeld & Nicolson, 1991.

Reynolds, K. & N. Humble. *Victorian heroines: representations of femininity in nineteenth-century literature and art.* Hemel Hempstead: Harvester Wheatsheaf, 1993.

Riegel, R. *American feminists.* Westport, Conn.: Greenwood Press, 1980.

Riley, D. *Am I that name? Feminism and the category of "women" in history.* London: Macmillan, 1988.

Riley, G. *Divorce, an American tradition.* New York: Oxford University Press, 1991.

Ripley, C. P. (ed.). *The black abolitionist papers, Volume I, The British Isles, 1830–1865.* Chapel Hill: University of North Carolina Press, 1985.

Roberts, B. *Those bloody women: three heroines of the Boer War.* London: John Murray, 1991.

Rogers, A. M. A. H. *Degrees by degrees: the story of the admission of Oxford women students to membership of the university.* Oxford: Oxford University Press, 1938.

Rose, S. O. *Limited livelihoods: gender and class in nineteenth-century England.* London: Routledge, 1992.

Rosen, A. *Rise up, women! The militant campaign of the Women's Social and Political Union, 1903–1914.* London: Routledge & Kegan Paul, 1994.

Rosenberg, R. *Beyond separate spheres: intellectual roots of modern feminism.* New Haven and London: Yale University Press, 1982.

Rothman. S. *Women's proper place: a history of changing ideals and practices, 1870 to the present.* New York: Basic Books, 1978.

Rover, C. *Women's suffrage and party politics in Britain, 1866–1914.* London: Routledge & Kegan Paul, 1967.

— *Love, morals and the feminists.* London: Routledge & Kegan Paul, 1970.

Rowan, C. Women in the Labour Party, 1906–1920. *Feminist Review* (12), 1982.

Rowbotham, S. *A new world for women: Stella Browne, socialist feminist.*

London: Pluto Press, 1977.

Rubinstein, D. *Before the suffragettes: women's emancipation in the 1890s.* Brighton: Harvester, 1986.

Rupp, L. Constructing internationalism: the case of transnational women's organizations, 1888–1945. *American Historical Review* 9, 1994.

Salem, D. C. *To better our world: black women in organized reform, 1890–1920.* Brooklyn, NY: Carlson Publishing, 1990.

Sánchez, G. J. "Go after the women": Americanization and the Mexican immigrant woman, 1915–1929. In *Unequal sisters: a multicultural reader in U.S. women's history*, V. L. Ruiz & E. C. DuBois (eds). New York and London: Routledge, 1994.

Scharf, L. *To work and to wed: female employment, feminism and the Great Depression.* Westport, Conn.: Greenwood Press, 1980.

Scharf, L. & J. M. Jensen. *Decades of discontent: the women's movement, 1920–1940.* Westport, Conn.: Greenwood Press, 1983.

Schneider, D. & C. J. Schneider. *American women in the Progressive Era.* New York: Facts on File, 1993.

Schreiner, O. *Women and labour.* London: T. Fisher Unwin, 1911.

Schwartz, J. *Radical feminists of heterodoxy: Greenwich Village, 1912–1940.* Norwich, Vt.: New Victoria, 1986.

Scott, A. F. *The southern lady: from pedestal to politics, 1830–1930.* Chicago: University of Chicago Press, 1970.

— *Natural allies: women's associations in American history.* Urbana and Chicago: University of Illinois Press, 1991.

Scott, A. F. & A. M. Scott. *One half of the people: the fight for woman suffrage.* Philadelphia, Pa: Lippincott, 1975.

Scott, J. W. *Gender and the politics of history.* New York: Columbia University Press, 1988.

Shanley, M. L. *Feminism, marriage, and the law in Victorian England, 1850–1895.* Princeton, NJ: Princeton University Press, 1989.

Shiman, L. L. *Women and leadership in nineteenth-century England.* London: Macmillan, 1992.

Showalter, E. *A literature of their own: from Charlotte Bronte to Doris Lessing.* London: Virago Press, 1978.

— *Sexual anarchy: gender and culture at the fin de siècle.* London: Virago Press, 1992.

Shryock, R. H. *Medical licensing in America, 1650–1965.* Baltimore, Md: Johns Hopkins University Press, 1972.

Simmons, C. Modern sexuality and the myth of Victorian repression. In *Gender and American history since 1890*, B. Melosh (ed.). London and New York: Routledge, 1993.

Sklar, K. K. Hull House as a community of women reformers in the 1890s. *Signs* 10, 1985.

— Women who speak for an entire nation: American and British women compared at the World Anti-Slavery Convention, London, 1840. *Pacific Historical Review* 59, 1990.

— The historical foundations of women's power in the creation of the American welfare state, 1830–1930. In *Mothers of a new world: maternalist politics and the origins of welfare states*, S. Koven & S. Michel (eds). London: Routledge, 1993.

— *Florence Kelly and the nation's work: the rise of women's political culture, 1830–1900*. New Haven, Conn.: Yale University Press, 1995.

Skocpol, T. *Protecting soldiers and mothers: the politics of social provision in the United States, 1870s–1920s*. Cambridge, Mass.: Belknap Press, 1992.

— *Social policy in the United States: future possibilities in historical perspective*. Princeton: Princeton University Press, 1995.

Smith, H. L. Sex vs class: British feminists and the Labour movement, 1919–29. *The Historian* 47, 1984.

Smith-Rosenberg, C. *Disorderly conduct: visions of gender in Victorian America*. New York: Oxford University Press, 1985.

Sochen, J. *The new woman: feminism in Greenwich Village, 1910–1920*. New York: Quadrangle Books, 1972.

Soldon, N. C. *Women in British Trade Unions, 1874–1976*. Dublin: Gill and Macmillan, 1978.

Solomon, B. M. *In the company of educated women: a history of women and higher education in America*. New Haven and London: Yale University Press, 1985.

Spender, D. & C. Hayman (eds). *How the vote was won and other suffragette plays*. London: Methuen, 1985.

Stansell, C. *City of women: sex and class in New York, 1789–1860*. New York: Alfred A. Knopf, 1986.

Stanton, E. C. *Eighty years and more: reminiscences, 1815–1897*. New York: T. Fisher Unwin, 1898. Reprinted in 1971 by Schocken.

Stanton, E. C. et al. (eds). *History of woman suffrage* [3 vols], 1881–6. New York: Fowler & Wells; vol. 4, 1902, Rochester NY: S. B. Anthony; vols 5–6, 1922, New York: J. J. Little & Ives.

Stearns, P. *Be a man! Males in modern society*. New York: Holmes & Meier, 1979.

Steinberg, R. *Wages and hours: labor and reform in twentieth century America*. New Brunswick, NJ: Rutgers University Press, 1982.

Steinson, B. J. *American women's activism in World War I*. New York: Garland, 1982.

Sterling, D. (ed.). *We are your sisters: black women in the nineteenth century*. New York and London: W. W. Norton, 1984.

Stetson, D. M. *A woman's issue: the politics of family law reform in England*. Westport, Conn.: Greenwood Press, 1982.

Stevens, D. *Jailed for freedom*. Freeport, NY: Books for Libraries Press, 1971. Originally published 1920.

Stock-Morton, P. Finding our own ways: different paths to women's history in the United States. In *Writing women's history: international perspectives*, K. Offen, R. R. Pierson, J. Rendall (eds.). London: Macmillan, 1991.

Stott, M. *Organisation women: the story of the National Union of Townswomen's Guilds*. London: Heinemann, 1978.

Strachey, R. *The cause: a short history of the women's movement in Great Britain*. London: Virago Press, 1978. Originally published 1928.

Strauss, S. *Traitors to the masculine cause: The men's campaigns for women's rights*. London: Greenwood Press, 1982.

Strobel, M. *European women and the second British empire*. Bloomington: Indiana University Press, 1991.

Stubbs, P. *Women and fiction: feminism and the novel, 1880–1920*. Brighton: Harvester, 1979.

Summers, A. A home from home – women's philanthropic work in the nineteenth century. In *Fit work for women*, S. Burman, (ed.). London: Croom Helm, 1979.

— *Angels and citizens: British women as military nurses, 1854–1914*. London: Routledge, 1988.

Sutherland, J. *Mrs Humphrey Ward: eminent Victorian, pre-eminent Edwardian*. Oxford: Oxford University Press, 1990.

Swanwick, H. M. *I have been young*. London: Victor Gollancz, 1935.

Talbot, M. & L. Rosenberry. *The history of the American Association of University Women*. Boston: Houghton Mifflin, 1931.

Tax, M. *The rising of women: feminist solidarity and class conflict, 1880–1917*. New York: Monthly Review Press, 1979.

Taylor, A. *Annie Besant: a biography*. Oxford University Press, 1992.

Taylor, B. *Eve and the new Jerusalem: socialism and feminism in the nineteenth century*. London: Virago, 1983.

Terborg-Penn, R. Discontented black feminists: prelude and postscript to the passage of the Nineteenth Amendment. In *Decades of discontent: the women's movement, 1920–1940*, L. Scharf & J. M. Jensen (eds). Westport, Conn.: Greenwood Press, 1983.

Thane, P. The women of the British Labour Party and feminism, 1906–45. In *British feminism in the twentieth century*, H. Smith (ed.). Aldershot: Edward Elgar, 1990.

— Women in the British Labour Party and the construction of state welfare, 1906–1939. In *Mothers of a new world: maternalist politics and the origins of welfare states*, S. Koven & S. Michel (eds). London: Routledge, 1993.

Thistlethwaite, F. *America and the Atlantic community: Anglo-American aspects, 1790–1850*. New York: Harper & Row, 1959.

Thomas, M. M. *The new woman in Alabama: social reforms and suffrage, 1890–1920.* Tuscaloosa: University of Alabama Press, 1992.

Tickner, L. *Spectacle of women: images of the suffrage campaign.* London: Chatto & Windus, 1989.

Trollope, J. *Britannia's daughters: women of the British Empire.* London: Pimlico, 1994.

Tulloch, G. *Mill and sexual equality.* Brighton: Harvester, 1984.

Tyack, D. & E. Hansot. *Learning together: a history of co-education in American schools.* New Haven: Yale University Press, 1990.

Tyrell, I. *Woman's world, woman's empire: the Woman's Christian Temperance Union in international perspective, 1880–1930.* Chapel Hill, NC: University Press of North Carolina, 1991.

Vicinus, M. *Independent women: work and community for single women, 1850–1920.* Chicago: Chicago University Press, 1985.

Vann Woodward, C. V. (ed.). *The comparative approach to American history.* New York: Basic Books, 1968.

Walker, L. Party political women: a comparative study of the Liberal women and the Primrose League, 1890–1914. In *Equal or different: women's politics, 1800–1914*, J. Rendall (ed.). Oxford: Blackwell, 1987.

Walkowitz, J. *Prostitution and Victorian society: women and the state.* Cambridge: Cambridge University Press, 1980.

— *City of dreadful delight: narratives of sexual danger in late-Victorian London.* London: Virago, 1992.

Walsh, M. R. *Doctors wanted, no women need apply: sexual barriers in the medical profession, 1835–1975.* New Haven, Conn. and London: Yale University Press, 1977.

Ware, S. *Beyond suffrage: women in the New Deal.* Cambridge, Mass.: Harvard University Press, 1981.

— *Holding their own: American women in the twentieth century.* Boston, Mass.: G. K. Hall, 1982.

— *Partner and I: Molly Dewson, feminism, and New Deal politics.* New Haven: Yale University Press, 1987.

Weeks, J. *Sex, politics and society: the regulation of sexuality since 1800.* London: Longman, 1981.

Weiss, N. *Farewell to the party of Lincoln: black politics in the age of FDR.* Princeton: Princeton University Press, 1983.

Wells, I. B. *Crusade for justice: the autobiography of Ida B. Wells.* Chicago and London: University of Chicago Press, 1970. A. M. Duster (ed.).

Wertheimer, B. M. *We were there.* New York, Pantheon, 1977.

Wheeler, M. S. *New women of the New South: the leaders of the woman suffrage movement in the southern states.* New York: Oxford University Press, 1993.

White, D. G. *Ar'n't I a woman? Female slaves in the plantation South*. New York: Norton, 1985.

Willard, F. E. *My happy half-century: the autobiography of an American woman*. London: Ward, Lock & Bourden, 1894.

Wilson, D. C. *Lone woman: the story of Elizabeth Blackwell, the first woman doctor*. Boston, Mass.: Little, Brown, 1970.

Winter, J. M. *The Great War and the British people*. London: Macmillan, 1985.

Woody, T. *A history of women's education in the United States* [2 vols]. New York: Octagon Books, 1966.

Wright, A. E. *The unexpurgated case against women's suffrage*. London: Constable, 1913.

Yans-McLaughlin, V. *Family and community: Italian immigrants in Buffalo, 1880–1930*. Ithaca, NY: Cornell University Press, 1977.

Yee, S. *Black women abolitionists: a study in activism, 1828–1860*. Knoxville: University of Tennessee Press, 1992.

Yellin, J. F. *Women and sisters: the anti-slavery feminists in American culture*. New Haven: Yale University Press, 1989.

Young, L. M. *In the public interest: the League of Women Voters, 1920–1970*. Westport, Conn.: Greenwood Press, 1989.

Yung, J. The social awakening of Chinese American women as reported in Chung Sai Yat Po, 1900–1911. In *Unequal sisters: a multi-cultural reader in U.S. women's history*, V. L. Ruiz & E. C. DuBois (eds). New York and London: Routledge, 1994.

Index